Stories NeverEnding

A Program Guide for Schools and Libraries

Stories NeverEnding

A Program Guide for Schools and Libraries

Jan Irving

Illustrations by Joni Giarratono

LIBRARIES
UNLIMITED
A Member of the Greenwood Publishing Group

Westport, Connecticut • London

Library of Congress Cataloging-in-Publication Data

Irving, Jan, 1942-
    Stories neverending : a program guide for schools and libraries / Jan Irving ; illustrations
by Joni Giarratono.
        p. cm.
    Includes bibliographical references and index.
    ISBN 1-56308-997-1 (pbk. : alk. paper)
    1. Storytelling—United States. 2. Elementary school libraries—Activity programs—United
States. 3. Children's libraries—Activity programs—United States. 4. Children—Books and
reading—United States. 5. Activity programs in education—United States. 6. Children's
stories—Bibliography. I. Title.
Z718.3.I787 2004
027.62'51—dc22   2003060487

British Library Cataloguing in Publication Data is available.

Library of Congress Catalog Card Number: 2003060487
ISBN: 1–56308–997–1

First published in 2004

Libraries Unlimited, 88 Post Road West, Westport, CT 06881
A Member of the Greenwood Publishing Group, Inc.
www.lu.com

Printed in the United States of America

The paper used in this book complies with the
Permanent Paper Standard issued by the National
Information Standards Organization (Z39.48–1984).

10   9   8   7   6   5   4   3   2   1

To Bill—
Loving husband, constant friend, and special editor
and
To the memory of my mother, Lois—natural storyteller
To the memory of my brother Gary—family wit and storyteller

with special thanks to Barbara Ittner, my publishing editor, for her
encouragement and insight

Contents

Introduction

Can you remember a time when there were no stories? Can you remember a time in your life when you did not know stories? Can you imagine how the first stories might have been told and passed on to other people? I cannot remember the "before story time" in my own life or in the world beyond, but I am intrigued by these questions.

When I was a library school student over twenty-five years ago, I made a slide show with accompanying music on the topic of the beginning of stories. The project consumed me. It began to take on a life of its own as I searched for the perfect music and visual images and reworked the text. I'm still proud of that project. Soon after the show was presented to class, I reworked it for a videotape series later used in a conference at the University of Iowa. More recently, I described the show to a colleague, who listened intently when I quoted the last lines of the tape. "As long as there are people to listen, stories will be told. Once upon a time.... Once there was and once there was not.... Snip, snap, snout, my tale's told out. And they lived happily ever after. Stories—the end is but the beginning." My friend listened then suggested I write a book titled *Stories Never End*. I accepted her challenge, and the book you hold in your hands is the result.

Stories are handed down through countless generations and seemingly take on lives of their own. Who knows where the stories we tell today will go? Stories live on and on through today's and tomorrow's tellers.

The never "endingness" of stories reminds me of each generation passing on the wisdom discovered in stories told to them by a preceding generation. Numerous chapters in the Bible use the narrative technique of naming a person who was "begat from, who was begat from, who was begat from."

If you have studied the history of storytelling and legend, you will agree that stories make us most human. Arthur Applebee's classic book *The Child's Concept of Story* explains that stories order the world for young children, and they pass on the values of a culture. As a librarian or teacher, this may sound so academic to you that you feel lost already. You may ask, "What does this mean to me as I go about my job of providing books to children? I really don't have time to wade through such heavy issues when I'm working to meet school standards."

This book may have grown from lofty-sounding ideals, but it is earth bound in a most practical way. My purpose is to introduce a range of books and related subject areas (art, poetry, math, food, and American history), literary genres and forms (humor, poetry), skills (storytelling, writing, booktalking), and concerns (motivating kids to read, building character). Linking children's literature to topics for learning is another way to extend the lives of stories.

The subjects covered here have proven to be of interest to elementary school–age children from kindergarten through Grade 6. The activities have been developed for both school and public libraries. You are encouraged to adapt and embellish these activities to your own needs and purposes. Each chapter follows the same organization. After an introduction to the subject area, I present a literature base—a bibliography of books from which I developed the programs and activities. Literature selections were based on availability in libraries. Most of the books in the bibliographies have been published in the past ten years, but many are classics from decades past. Each chapter includes at least two full-scale programs, one appropriate for a public library and the other for a school setting. With a few minor adjustments, these programs may be used in either setting. Idea springboards end the chapters with additional activities that you can develop on your own.

My core belief that stories and books have the ability to connect all disciplines is woven throughout the text. The phrase "literature across the curriculum" expresses this belief. This philosophy has been an educational trend for more than a decade, but I believe it is more than a fad. It communicates to me the importance of interconnecting story with all areas of learning.

Research has proposed that people learn differently because we all possess different intellectual strengths. This theory of multiple intelligences was developed by Dr. Howard Gardner, a professor at Harvard University. Teachers and librarians who are aware of this information can select books to help children who have different focuses and diverse strengths. Although I have not used Gardener's terms explicitly, the programs address the following categories: math-logic intelligence, verbal-linguistic intelligence, spatial intelligence (visual learning), musical intelligence, body-kinesthetic intelligence, interpersonal intelligence, and intrapersonal intelligence. (Consult the bibliography at the end of this book to learn more about the theory of multiple intelligences and its applications.)

If you are overworked and under a tight budget but still excited about providing good books and new ideas to the kids in your community, please read on. It is you, as an educator, librarian, or parent, who can breathe new life into stories for today's children. As you work with children and literature, you'll undoubtedly witness the power of stories. Perhaps you'll even agree with me that stories are truly never ending.

And now, may we all lift our voices to the stories around us to create a world of new understanding for the children of today and tomorrow.

—Jan Irving, youth librarian, teacher, writer, and storyteller

1

Red Hot Readers

Reading Incentive Programs and Books about Books

Summer reading programs in America's public libraries have long been the main ring of the library circus. I remember reading forty books one summer during my own childhood so that I could receive a small wooden chunk painted gold to represent gold bouillon in a "Gold Rush" summer reading program. What a far cry from the pricey incentives given today! The reality is that libraries compete with dozens of commercial programs, from Pizza Hut's "Book It," McDonald's "All-American Reading Challenge," and the Toys 'R' Us "Geoffrey's Reading Railroad." Other businesses can offer even larger material rewards. Critics of reading for "bribes" remind educators and parents that food coupons or the enticing products result in reading for the reward rather than learning that reading is its own reward. Moreover, some critics maintain that such reading incentive programs actually turn kids into worse readers.

Most researchers tell us the one prize found to be effective in promoting "the reading habit" is the reward of a book itself. Approach local service clubs such as Rotary, Lions Club, or the professional organizations of educators, doctors, or attorneys to request money to purchase bulk paperback books—these are excellent rewards to promote reading. Parents and kids alike appreciate this kind of incentive.

Research tells us that reading as a leisure-time activity is decreasing at alarming rates. As a result of the hours spent playing computer games and watching television rather than choosing to read, children in upper elementary schools have more limited vocabularies and confine their reading to class assignments.

Public librarians observe kids playing computer and card games in libraries after school, as if they had been given no homework assignments. Many parents check out videos to entertain children rather than good books to read aloud with their families.

What can librarians do to promote reading, and possibly to help children develop a lifelong reading habit? Summer reading programs are known to raise children's reading levels or, at least, to help them maintain the reading levels they achieved at the end of school. Year-round reading programs at public libraries reinforce the skills that children learn in schools.

The focus of this chapter is on promoting reading through methods other than material rewards. Specifically, it can help you promote reading by sharing the joy of good books. It suggests themes for reading programs and supplies scripts and ideas for marketing and displaying appealing books. Chapter 8 discusses doing booktalks and teaching older children to booktalk for their peers. This activity works well to motivate older children to read titles they might not discover on their own. Such approaches are especially useful for Children's Book Week and parents' night at schools. Logos for reading themes and patterns for skits that promote reading are also included.

The bibliography in this chapter includes resources on reading, books, and libraries. In addition, the bibliography at the end of the book lists professional titles to guide the teacher or librarian. Fully developed programs are included in the chapter, as well as springboards to assist you in developing your own ideas.

Books about Books, Reading, and Libraries

Bloom, Becky. *Wolf!* Illus. Pascal Biet. Orchard, 1999.

A hungry wolf comes to town and visits a farm to fill his stomach. But this is an unusual farm, one for educated animals. Pig, Cow, and Duck are only interested in reading, so Wolf goes to a library, school, and bookstore to learn to read. The animals now pay attention to the wolf, who joins their storytelling troupe. Great for storytelling and reading aloud to all ages!

Bruss, Deborah. *Book! Book! Book!* Illus. Tiphanie Beeke. Scholastic, 2001.

The farm animals are bored when the children go back to school. Making a parade to the library, the animals can't communicate with the librarian until hen clucks "Book! Book! Book!" Use this book to promote reading during Children's Book Week by holding your own book parade. (See Reading Promotion Activities later in this chapter.)

Deedy, Carmen Agra. *The Library Dragon.* Illus. Michael White. Peachtree, 1994.

Sunrise Elementary School has a real dragon for a librarian. She keeps books away from children's greasy fingers, scorches the principal, and discourages teachers. When Molly Brickmeyer wanders into the library, she changes Dragon Lady Scales into the heartwarming librarian Miss Lotty, who then transforms the whole library scene.

Ernst, Lisa Campbell. *Stella LouElla's Runaway Book.* Simon and Schuster, 1998.

When Stella LouElla loses her library book, she embarks on a wild trek around town to retrace her steps. Finally, she goes to the library to confess the loss. The story ends happily with Stella checking out a new book. The rest of the community follow her lead by checking out books and parading out of the library into town. Ernst's lively illustrations and story will encourage children to retell the story.

Faulkner, Keith. *The Monster Who Loved Books.* Illus. Jonathan Lambert. Orchard, Scholastic, 2002.

While reading in his father's bookstore, Bradley discovers a monster busily eating the books. The boy shows the monster the adventures inside books. In the end, Bradley awakens from his bed and wonders if he really did meet a monster who learned to become a book lover. The pop-up illustrations and clever text will win over younger students and will also have appeal for kids who love monster stories.

Polacco, Patricia. *The Bee Tree.* Philomel, Putnam, 1993.

Grandpa and Mary Ellen chase a bee they lost from a jar, until they reach its hive. A fun-loving crowd of people follow their chase. Back home, Grandpa tells Mary Ellen, a reluctant reader, that she can find sweetness inside of books, much like the sweet honey they found. In the end, Mary Ellen becomes a book lover, too. Polacco's storytelling skills combine with her exuberant illustrations to celebrate the joy of reading—even reluctant readers will be urged on in their reading.

Scieszka, Jon. *The Stinky Cheese Man and Other Fairly Stupid Tales.* Illus. Lane Smith. Viking Penguin, 1992.

This Caldecott Honor Book is a perfect marriage of wacky fairy tales and avant-garde illustrations. Children will be introduced to the parts of a book through bossy Little Red Hen and Jack, the narrator. Somehow, the Title Page and Table of Contents are able to interrupt these two strong characters. Near the end of the story, Red Hen is gobbled up by the giant just as Jack announces "The End." Read, retell, and act out this story for kids of all ages.

Williams, Suzanne. *Library Lil.* Illus. Steven Kellogg. Dial Books for Young Readers, 1997.

Anyone who thinks librarians are wimps needs to meet the adventurous Lil. When the frisky little girl grows up to take a job as a librarian in Chesterville, she shakes up the once-resistant readers, transforming them into avid book lovers. Her bookmobile and story times bring in the crowds—even motorcycle tough guys become bookworms!

Reading Promotion Activities

A *Book! Book! Book!* Parade

This activity is perfect to use for parent's night in school libraries or story time at public libraries; it is designed for several age groups or for a family story night. Older children can perform the story for primary students. Because the program includes reading, acting, and artistic projects, it will appeal to verbal, visual, and kinesthetic learning styles.

Materials Needed

1. A copy each of Deborah Bruss's *Book! Book! Book!* and Becky Bloom's *Wolf!* (see book list for details)

2. Paper, scissors, and elastic for the animal masks shown in this chapter (Figs. 1.1–1.5)

3. Mask faces prepared by enlarging the patterns (Figs. 1.1–1.5) on a photocopier; puppet heads made by copying the patterns (Figs. 1.6–1.9) onto heavy paper

4. Craft sticks

5. Posterboard and markers

6. Dowels for pennants or book banners

Procedure

1. Prepare by photocopying Figures 1.1–1.5, enlarged sufficiently to create masks. Assemble the masks for all children involved in the project (older children can take part in this), and make copies of the script for the older ones.

2. Either read aloud or tell Bruss's book *Book! Book! Book!* Then introduce the characters of Cow, Goat, Pig, Duck, and Hen. Tell the audience that these characters have come to promote some of their favorite books in the library.

3. Have the children don their masks. The librarian begins by asking all the characters to introduce themselves and tell the audience about their favorite book.

4. Older children then read the script (they may also memorize the script ahead of time). With younger ones, read the lines aloud, and then have the children repeat them. For author names that may be difficult to pronounce, have older children practice the pronunciation first. For younger children, simply use the book titles. Once they have finished, thank all the animals and display copies of the books mentioned on the table in the story corner.

Figure 1.1

Figure 1.2

Figure 1.3

Figure 1.4

Figure 1.5

Book Parade Script

Cow: Hello. You didn't expect me to say "moo," did you? You see, I'm an educated cow, so my favorite book is *Wolf!* by Becky Bloom. Read this if you think cows only chew grass. We also read books! Don't believe it? Read *Wolf!*

Goat: I'm Goat, so I like stories about goats, of course. One of the best is *The Three Billy Goats Gruff,* retold by Marcia Brown. We goats are not all alike. Some of us are big, and some of us are small. The goats in this story are brave. They overcome an ugly old troll. Actually, I like the troll in this story because he is soooo ugly. How ugly? Read this book, and you'll find out for yourself.

Pig: I love reading because there are so many books with pigs in them. You might say I "pig out" on books! But my very favorite is *The True Story of the Three Little Pigs* by Jon Scieszka and Lane Smith. I don't know why I like this book, because the wolf tells this story—and he tells it all wrong! You will laugh, but listen to me. Don't trust the wolf. He's the bad guy!

Duck: I've just gone "quackers" for *Make Way for Ducklings* by Robert McCloskey. Did you know ducks can stop traffic in big cities? This famous book describes a duck parade across a busy street in Boston. They tell me that there's now a statue of ducks in Boston in honor of this book. Isn't that ducky?

Hen: Hello, I'm the famous Little Red Hen. I know you've read about me in the story "The Little Red Hen." Paul Galdone has made a book about this very old story. The book shows that hens can do anything, even if no one helps them. But I want to tell you about another wacky book by those two fun guys, Jon Scieszka and Lane Smith. The name of the book is *The Stinky Cheese Man,* and it's packed with fractured fairy tales. I'm the real star of the book because I appear on the first page. You'll see how important I am if you read this cool book!

5. Next, read the book *Wolf!* After you've finished the story, ask children to take the parts of Wolf, Duck, Pig, and Cow. The children select stick puppets made from the illustrations in this chapter (Figs. 1.6–1.9). The animal faces have been mounted on craft sticks. Each child inserts the character stick puppet into a book and then holds up the book so that the animal puppet will cover the child's face. As the story proceeds, the sight of animal heads popping over the books will look to the audience as if the animals are reading.

6. As you read the book, you might direct the animals to move, corresponding with action in the story. For example, in the story, when the wolf leaves, the other animals to go to the library, school, and bookstore; the child playing the wolf may move away from the group at this point, and then move back as he returns to the farm.

7. As a culminating activity, give children paper and posterboard to make their own book banners or posters in the spirit of the Bruss's *Book! Book! Book!* After the posters are made, lead the children in a book parade around the room. One by one, each child reads aloud the slogan on their poster. Everyone cheers after each child reads. Following are some ideas for slogans written as if different animals were promoting reading.

> "I quack for books." (Duck)
>
> "Chew on a Good Book." (Cow or Goat)
>
> "Books MOOVE me." (Cow)
>
> "Don't horse around—Read Books!" (Horse)
>
> "Pig Out on Books." (Pig)
>
> "I just eat up books." (Goat)
>
> "Don't chicken out—Read those books!" (Hen)

8. Display the signs around the room, or let children take them home as a souvenir. Provide a variety of bookmarks and plastic book bags for take-home items.

Reading Programs All Year Round

During the summer, local public libraries often adopt the themes of state library reading programs. School's summer reading programs often coordinate their reading lessons with ideas from the public library. Here's a great way to promote your library reading programs that can be adapted to any program theme you choose. (A list of theme suggestions is provided, but use your imagination.)

Materials Needed

1. Posters made by library staff or children to promote the program; commercially produced posters can also be used

2. Reading logs made from colored paper with space for children to list the book titles they read during the summer

3. A display wall with cutouts of animals or objects appropriate to the theme.

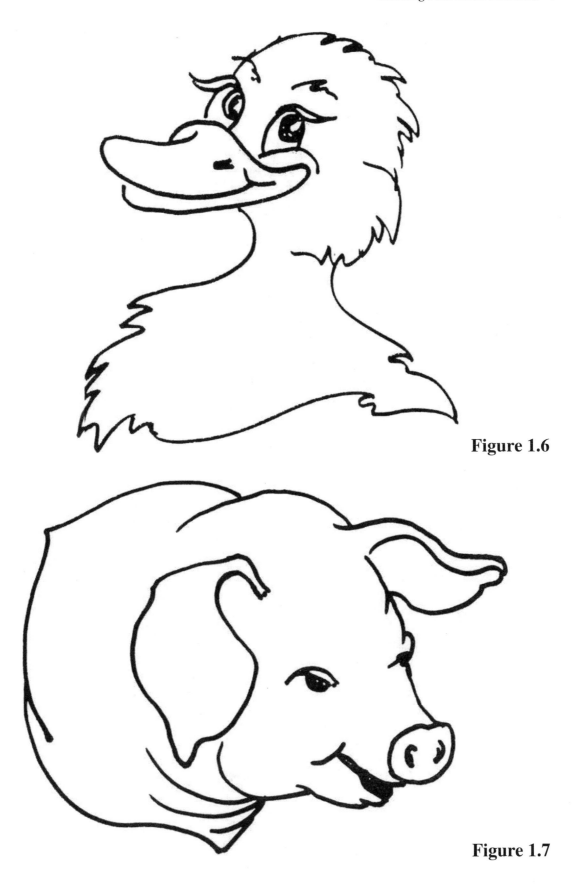

Figure 1.6

Figure 1.7

Figure 1.8

Figure 1.9

Procedure

1. Decorate the room with posters and supply reading logs to children.

2. Each child who participates writes his or her name on the shape. *Note that numbers of books read are not displayed in public, only the names of participants.*

3. If you wish to develop your own theme, consider these ideas:

   - What local events, places, or products might link the library with the local community? For example, a town with a railroad museum could use a theme such as "Ride the Reading Railroad" or "Conduct Me to Your Readers."

   - Think of real or fantastic animals with child appeal. Brainstorm phrases or idioms associated with those animals. Here are some examples:

     "Get MOOvin' . . . Read 'til the Cows Come Home"

     "Dragonsummer"

     "Read! It's the Cat's Meow. Wow!"

   - Think about hobbies, popular media, and things that kids love, then make up slogans. For example:

     "Run Circles 'Round the Reading Game"

     "Tune into the Book Station" (Use headphones and radios for visuals)

     "Read-opoly! The Best Game in Town"

Sample Fall Program: Red Hot Readers

Chili peppers, popular in the Southwest, have become a favorite in other places as well. Fast-food Mexican restaurants use the chili pepper motif, so children will be familiar with this symbol.

Materials Needed

1. Red, green, and black construction paper for the dancing peppers

2. Patterns in this chapter (Figs. 1.10 and 1.11)

3. Red fabric and green ribbon for the chili pepper pillow

4. Fiberfill to stuff the fabric peppers

5. Plastic google eyes (optional)

6. Snacks (tortilla chips and salsa)

Procedure

1. Have children or library staff make dancing chili peppers for wall decorations using the pattern in this chapter (Fig. 1.10).

2. Make a chili pepper pillow. Ask teen or parent volunteers to help prepare materials to save staff time. Enlarge the pattern (Fig. 1.11) in this chapter to the size of a commercial neck pillow. Cut out fabric using the pattern. Sew up the pepper, leaving enough space to stuff the fabric pepper with fiberfill. Hand stitch the opening to close it. Tie green ribbon around the stem to resemble leaves. These pepper pillows can be given away for prize drawings or simply hung around the room.

Figure 1.10

Figure 1.11

3. Make reading logs from construction paper for children to write down titles of the books they read. If you have enough volunteer assistance, consider cutting the paper into the shape of a chili pepper.

4. Conclude the fall reading program with a family reading night. If you have enough pepper pillows, give these away to families who attend. Welcome the families by reading or telling a story about families and reading such as Patricia Polacco's *The Bee Tree*. Fill a book cart, a red wagon, or any other "vehicle" you can find with books, especially books about families, and invite participants to choose a book to read together. *(Note: You may need to move families to different parts of the room or in study rooms because of the noise.)* Bring the group together after ten or fifteen minutes. Ask if anyone would like to read their book aloud to the whole group. Each family member could read a page of a book then pass it to the next family member to read so that the book reading becomes lively and interactive. Conclude the family reading night by serving tortilla chips and various salsa dips.

Sample Winter Program: "Groundhog Readers Club"

Many people are fascinated by America's mascot groundhog in Pennsylvania, Punxsutawney Phil, who supposedly predicts how long winter will continue by whether he sees his shadow when he emerges from his hole. The groundhog symbol represents holing up for the winter, and, in this case, kid groundhog readers will be cuddling up with good books. Many libraries have used this winter reading program, but some fun new details will give you a fresh slant on the theme.

Materials Needed

1. A groundhog costume or groundhog puppet to appear weekly throughout the program

2. Photocopies scripts for children, such as the one included here, to promote specific books

3. Snacks (peanut-butter balls rolled in broken bits of pretzel to resemble groundhogs)

4. Construction-paper reading logs for children to record the books they have read

5. Photocopies of the groundhog illustration in this chapter (Fig. 1.12) to decorate the room and use as a logo on the reading log

6. Video recording equipment to record the program, if desired

Procedure

1. Dress up a child in the groundhog costume or use the groundhog puppet to answer the interviewer's questions.

2. Select a child or staff member to interview the groundhog. The "Groundhog's Interview" script will guide you, but children may want to make up their own questions for the groundhog puppet to answer. The idea is for the groundhog to promote new books for children to read each week.

3. Serve peanut-butter groundhogs and view the videotape if you have made one.

4. For the next session, invite a local weather forecaster to tell children how weather is predicted. Record the presentation on video, if desired. Display books about weather.

5. During one week of the reading program, invite a science teacher to do a weather-related science activity. This session could also be videotaped. This public library event will motivate children's school science projects.

Figure 1.12

Groundhog's Interview

Interviewer: Good morning, Great Groundhog. I understand that you have some reading suggestions for kids in the audience today.

GG: Yes! I just finished a clever book called *Cloudy with a Chance of Meatballs* by Judi Barrett.

I: Hasn't that book been around for awhile?

GG: Why, yes, but you know I read it once or twice every year. I just love all the food jokes in the pictures. And the name of the town where the story takes place is Chewandswallow. Isn't that a great name?

I: I agree. Don't you think the author should write a sequel?

GG: She did! That one's called *Pickles over Pittsburgh*.

I: I missed that one. What else is good to read?

GG: Well since we were talking about weather-related food stories, let me recommend *The Rain Came Down* by David Shannon. It tells about all the things that can happen when it rains.

I: Such as?

GG: A painter can't paint the outside of a building. The rain causes a leak in the roof of a bakery so the baker's cakes get wet. People get into arguments.

I: Does it stop?

GG: Of course rain stops. But you'll have to read the book to find out about the happy ending!

I: OK, I will. What else?

GG: Speaking of rain not stopping, I did read a fascinating book about a flood called *The Great Midwest Flood* by Carole Vogel. This flood happened back in the summer of 1993, and the rain went on for months! Graves were unearthed and some coffins in Missouri washed downstream. The city of Des Moines, Iowa, lost its water supply.

I: Did it rain cats and dogs?

GG: No, silly. But that reminds me of a story by Joe Hayes. It's called "The Day It Snowed Tortillas."

I: You must be kidding.

GG: Read Joe's story in the story collection by the same name to find out.

I: You keep saying "read it to find out." Are you trying to tell me something?

GG: Yes, I am. Go to the library and read. Check out the weather books! Check out the stories about weather! Check out anything that interests you, but read, and come back next week. I'll be talking about books on animals like me. Everybody loves to read about animals.

Sample Spring Reading Program: "Purple People Readers"

Many adults may remember the popular song "Purple People Eaters," which inspired the title of this reading program. Children enjoy the word play, the alliteration, and the idea of purple people or purple creatures reading books. The following details will help you create your own spring program, one that is more off beat than the overused ideas of flowers, butterflies, and gardens. Children will welcome this new twist.

Materials Needed:

1. Photocopies on purple paper (enlarged, if desired) of the monsters illustrated in this chapter (Figs. 1.13–1.15)

2. Copies of the purple people readers for children to take home and add their own details

3. Displays of books on monsters, real and imagined; on fantasy creatures; and on books using the word "purple"

Procedure

1. Reproduce images of the various purple people readers in this chapter (Figs. 1.13–1.15) for wall decorations on a photocopier; enlarge if desired.

2. Reproduce monster pictures on white paper and provide colored markers for children to individualize their own people readers.

3. Create book displays around the theme as well as books using the word "purple" in the title.

4. Hold an opening or concluding event to motivate readers. Retell the stories of favorite monster books, such as *Where the Wild Things Are,* with children making monster sounds and actions as the story is told. Read other monster books or challenge children to find books on the library shelves that use a color in the title.

5. Serve purple food to the group, such as purple grapes or grape jelly sandwiches.

Figure 1.13

Figure 1.14

Figure 1.15

Idea Springboards: Activities to Develop

"Book-mercials"

Did you ever do a mini booktalk of just a few sentences to promote a favorite title? Then you were doing what I call a "book-mercial"! Compose a couple of lively sentences for written, oral, or e-mail sharing. Nothing promotes reading more than "word of mouth" advertising. Here are a few examples written in "kid style," as if an elementary-age student might be creating the "mercials" for other kids. Draft kids in your classroom or library program to read these book-mercials. Then pass out index cards for everyone to write their own "mercials."

If you think you hate to write poetry, then you'll like *Love That Dog* by Sharon Creech. It's a "quick read" and will make you laugh. You may think you don't like poetry, but I know this book will change your mind.

My mom always tried to make me read books from the library during the summer. I just wanted to swim or goof off, but then I found this weird book by Jon Scieszka called *Summer Reading Is Killing Me*. It was funny, and I liked it a lot.

I like cartoons and I like funny books. That's why I'm reading all these books by Dav Pilkey. The main character has this name my mom hates. His name is Captain Underpants. Hey! All the Captain Underpants books are great.

One of my favorite books is *That's Good That's Bad*. I read it two years ago. You know, it has all those funny things like falling out of an airplane, and it ends up being good not bad. I'm excited Margery Cuyler has written a new one called *That's Good! That's Bad in the Grand Canyon*. It's cool.

I visited my grandmother last summer, and she took me to the Butterfly Pavilion near Denver, Colorado. She also bought me this book to take home so I could learn more about butterflies. It's called *Becoming Butterflies* by Anne Rockwell and I love it.

Write Your Very Own Reading Songs

Remember the old folk songs you learned when you were young? Make up your own versions of them with a reading theme. "Here We Go 'Round the Mulberry Bush" might become "Here We Go 'Round the Reading Tree." "Mary Had a Little Lamb" could become "We All Like Our Library Books." "Today Is Monday" could keep the same title, but choose a category of books to read each day of the week. Following is my version.

Today is Monday
Today is Monday
Monday Mysteries
Read a book today.
Today is Tuesday
Today is Tuesday
Tuesday Poetry
Monday Mysteries
Read two books today.
Today is Wednesday
Today is Wednesday
Wednesday Biography

Tuesday Poetry
Monday Mysteries
Read three books today.
Today is Thursday
Today is Thursday
Thursday Sports Stars
Wednesday Biography
Tuesday Poetry
Monday Mysteries
Read four books today.
Today is Friday
Today is Friday
Friday Fantasy
Thursday Sports Stars
Wednesday Biography
Tuesday Poetry
Monday Mysteries
Read five books today!

Of course you will want to have a sing-a-long program with kids singing their own original songs. Set up a display of music books and collections of songs for everyone to check out.

The Runaway Library Book Chase

Lisa Campbell Ernst's *Stella LouElla's Runaway Book* is about the child who goes on a chase to find an-almost-overdue library book. This theme will be a familiar, although perhaps exaggerated, situation for many children. Act out this story, adding your own touches. I have found children can do this more easily if you orally go through all the episodes in the story after you read the book. This would be my "prompt."

Prompt for Acting Out Stella Louella's Runaway Book

Let's go back to the book, looking at the pictures, so we can remember all the places Stella looks for her lost library book.

1.   She looks in the closets.

2.   She looks on shelves.

3.   She looks in beds, baskets, and bathtubs (three "B" places). What are they again?

4.   She looks in toy boxes, tool boxes, and cereal boxes (three boxes). What kinds?

Continue through the rest of the book so everyone can remember where to go. Assign each child a different location to look when acting out the story. Then switch parts so several children can walk through the story.

For an alternative activity, ask children to retell their own runaway library book sequence by discussing other places to look—in the microwave, inside the refrigerator, in the family car, at a friend's house, in a school desk, and maybe the public library book was accidentally returned to just the right place—the school library!

Sandwich Board Advertisements

Introduce children to sandwich boards. In times past, "the Sandwich Man" wore two large boards hinged at the top by straps for wearing over the shoulders. As he walked down the street, people read his announcements.

Cut out pieces of posterboard similar to the illustration in this chapter (Fig. 1.16). Ask children to write their own book advertisements on the boards and wear them as they walk down the hall or around the library, promoting favorite books. The boards can be draped over easels as a display at the entrance to the library. Children can make mini sandwich board notebooks to keep for book diaries.

Reading Tricks or Tricky Ways to Capture Readers (When They Least Suspect It)

Do you have a reluctant reader in your room or in your home? My son didn't check out library books once he was reading on his own. How could this be? As a children's librarian, I was frustrated. I had read to him from the beginning. I brought home piles of new books. Did he read? I watched. Yes, he was reading—the home encyclopedia!

Most children who are read to will become readers on their own, but not always. Sometimes we succeed because we have come through difficult situations. Take heart.

The following lists of suggestions have been set up as two bookmarks. Photocopy these samples to share with parents in your school or library.

Figure 1.16   **Figure 1.17**

Tricky Ways to Capture Readers

1. Read yourself. Set a good example.

2. Read aloud to your kids—books, jokes, recipes, ads, anything!

3. Leave notes for children so they will be extra motivated to read.

4. Casually leave books with great looking covers around the house.

5. Read the same picture book five days in a row. Children love repetition. Read the book until the child "reads" it back to you!

6. Hug your child. If you are a teacher, smile at the child. Read a short book. Hug your child again. Little "book hugs" encourage reading better than nagging.

7. Read aloud with verve and expression! Make the reading so electric that kids will think you are more talented than a TV star. Keep your reading voice in tune!

8. Read "offbeat" books. Read books with wacky illustrations or curious titles, read riddle books, and, yes, try reading poetry by Bruce Lansky, Jack Prelutsky, Shel Silverstein, Doug Florian.

9. Keep a book in your shopping bag or briefcase so you can read anywhere.

10. Collect a group of everyday items with writing on them. Your list might include bus schedules, menus, recipes, directions for playing a game, movie tickets. Make a poster to hang in the kitchen titled, "Why Read?"

More Tricky Ways to Capture Readers

1. Give a book in place of an electronic toy. Toys become dated. Books do not.

2. Read to the dog or cat. Perhaps your child will listen, too.

3. Find a reading chair. Place a basket of books nearby. Invite your child to snuggle up and read with you.

4. Place an easy chair or carpet squares around the room so they are ready when you announce "DEAR" (Drop everything and read).

5. Buy or make book postcards. Book publishers will send these to you. Pictures of book characters or book covers are shown on one side. Ask kids to record their favorite quotes from the book on the other side.

6. Use "book words" in your conversation.

   "I'm feeling Eeyore-ish today, aren't you?"

   "Isn't today Mudluscious!"

   "You're a real Maniac McGee!"

7. Sing books! Make up tunes for poems, titles of books. Ask kids to sing riddles with you!

8. Turn out the lights and tell scary stories or episodes from classics. Who wouldn't want to hear about Odysseus putting out the eye of the Cyclops from *The Odyssey*? Tell the stories in your own words in the oral tradition.

9. Unplug the television.

10. Leave cookies, milk, and books for Santa Claus. Read scary stories on Halloween eve. Put small books in Easter baskets. Read stories about colonial times on the Fourth of July. Celebrate books on holidays throughout the year!

Art Smarts

Books about Art and Artists with Hands-On Activities

Imagine that you are enrolled in a daylong workshop titled "Paint or Die." Just reading the title of the workshop inspired you enough to devote half of your already busy weekend to paint. You have been caught up with so many details on your job that your free spirit is waning. You feel something like Tinkerbell in James Barrie's play *Peter Pan*. Remember the line in the play that implores the audience to clap if you believe in fairies? You know you need to clap to keep the tiny sprite alive. You know you must do this art retreat.

Once inside the artist's garage-shed workshop, you and the other participants are asked to remain completely silent all day. You think, "I will die. Whenever I am distressed I have to talk!" But you respect the silence that will stretch before you for six whole hours.

Soon the quiet surrounds you as you begin to notice that this is a healing place. Carefully spaced spotlights dramatize large sheets of paper thumb-tacked to whitewashed walls. You are handed a brush and led to a table laden with pots of intense shades of tempera paint. No instructions or limits are given. In a quiet voice, the instructor invites you to paint your heart out, to paint from deep down inside of yourself.

You swirl magenta around teal clouds circled by forest green vines that blossom into buttercups. You splash wild strawberry veins across Prussian blue blobs. At the end of six hours, you are exhausted but renewed. This is a true story. It happened one day to me.

Perhaps you remember painting as a child. If you were lucky, you had art classes in school and were allowed to use any and all the colors to create your own pictures. You lost yourself in your work. You were in "the flow," a heightened sense of your senses. You were a free spirit.

The point of these stories is that you as a librarian or teacher need to lose yourself in art and give the children you teach the permission, time, and space to experience art for themselves. Schools all over the country during these tight economic times have dropped art teachers and limited art programs. Often only children from affluent families have the opportunity to take art lessons or go to museums where they are exposed to art.

In my own teaching career, I learned that sometimes "at-risk" students blossom through art and creative expression. In my library world, I have seen unruly kids become calm in after-school programs when they were given opportunities to create art.

Fortunately, many book publishers have been bringing us glorious biographies about artists and publishing clever stories with children of today meeting artists from past times. The covers and inside pages of these books could be hung in an art museum. In one of Laurence Anholt's books, a girl named Camille meets a strange man who arrives in her town. He has no friends, but he paints sunflowers. In a picture book by James Mayhew, a girl named Katie goes to an art museum with her grandmother one rainy day. She reaches into a painting and touches a vase of sunflowers that spill onto the floor. Art crashes into our world, and we are never the same again.

Unless your school or library has a strong arts program, children may need your special guidance to lead them to these books. Read them, booktalk them, open up the pages and enjoy. Then follow up your reading with open-ended art projects for children. I wouldn't go as far as one of my former colleagues when she pronounced, "No patterns, no model projects—nothing to inhibit what the child will express on her own!" I use sample projects to guide children, but I don't give out coloring sheets or "paint-by-number" projects. I also believe one of the best gifts you can give children is to teach them to talk about visuals using precise words.

I remember one of Betsy Hearne's workshops in which she urged the group to eliminate the words "cute" and "colorful" from our vocabulary. She taught us to use expressive, specific words with children so that they, too, will see "sepia tones" or "angular lines." "Cute" may be appropriate to describe a Disney bunny, a case in which one bunny looks like the next bunny. "Cute" may apply to a Disney Snow White who looks much like a Disney Cinderella or a Disney Sleeping Beauty. "Cute" does not describe Nancy Ekholm Burkett's delicate Snow White nor Paul Zindel's northern Italian Rapunzel. "Sloppy words," said one of my college English literature professors, "are the mark of a sloppy mind." Precise language helps children think more clearly.

The year I served on the Caldecott committee, I was grateful for the ability to discuss art in children's books as thoughtfully as I could. During the past decade, publishers have supplied information about art media and techniques opposite the title page of many picture books. Astute teachers and librarians point out this information to students.

Don't worry what the school administration will think if you do art in the school library. Rest easy. If the principal asks exactly what skills are children learning to satisfy school standards when you share art books and make mobiles, use the following list.

Children learn these skills through art:

1. Hand-to-eye coordination

2. Refinement of small motor skills

3. Shape relationship and the ability to visualize spatially (architects, mathematicians, and scientists need these skills)

4. Pattern recognition

5. Imaginative thinking

Remember also that educators enlightened by Gardner's theory of multiple intelligences know to include visual-spatial approaches in their teaching. This chapter provides projects useful in this area.

Of course, you and I know we are really doing something more. We are letting children search, explore, express, and learn to see. We are exposing them to a world where they will want to look and think in new ways.

The following books about art and artists will serve as springboards to begin your discovery into art through children's books.

Books about Art and Artists

Anholt, Laurence. *Camille and the Sunflowers.* Barrons, 1984.

Camille, a young boy, meets the artist Van Gogh, who has just moved to town. The boy names Vincent the "Sunflower Man," and they become great friends. Camille even dreams about the artist painting a starry night. Anholt fictionalizes the story but adds insets of some of Van Gogh's own paintings to add to the authenticity.

Anholt, Laurence. *Degas and the Little Dancer: A Story about Edgar Degas.*
  Barrons, 1996.
  A young girl, Marie, dreams of becoming a dancer. To afford dancing lessons, she poses for Degas, the famous artist. When the sculpture is finished, Marie gives him her peach-colored hair ribbon, which he incorporates into the statue. Although Anholt creates the story about Marie, details about the artist are based on fact.

Anholt, Laurence. *Leonardo and the Flying Boy: A Story about Leonardo da Vinci.* Barrons, 1996.
  The Renaissance artist Leonardo da Vinci takes on several boy apprentices, who delight in seeing his paintings and flying machine. Based on fragments of historical accounts, the book incorporates Anholt's paintings as well as renderings of Leonardo's works.

Anholt, Laurence. *Picasso and the Girl with a Ponytail: A Story about Pablo Picasso.* Barrons, 1998.
  Picasso paints a portrait of Sylvette, a girl with a ponytail, and as his work progresses, he abstracts the painting and then turns it into a sculpture. Based on a true story, Anholt adds drawings in the style of the famous artist. The back endpapers of the book are photographs of the girl and the artist as they really were.

Bucks, Brad, and Joan Holub. *Vincent van Gogh, Sunflowers and Swirly Stars.* Grosset & Dunlap, 2001.
  The story of Vincent's life is told in first person from a child's point of view, with numerous whimsical cartoons as well as reproductions from the famous artist's works. Those works include the picture of the yellow house, sunflowers, the starry night, and his bedroom.

Duggleby, John. *Artist in Overalls: The Life of Grant Wood.* Chronicle, 1996.
  The story of Grant Wood's life and art includes photographs, colored reproductions of his paintings, and an art lesson at the end of the book.

Hersey, Bob. *Van Gogh's House: A Pop-Up Experience.* Universe, 1998.
  Brief text accompanies an enchanting three-dimensional pop-up display of the interior of the famous yellow house. Little standup figures of Van Gogh and others will inspire children to create stories about the artist and his life.

Johnson, Keesia, and Jane O'Connor. *Henri Matisse: Drawing with Scissors.* Grosset & Dunlap, 2002.
  Photographs, reproductions of Matisse paintings, and lively colored illustrations tell the story of the artist's life. Instructions for making your own color cutouts are included.

Le Tord, Bijou. *A Bird or Two: A Story about Henri Matisse.* Eerdmans Books for Young Readers, 1999.
  With paintings and cutouts in the style of Matisse, Le Tord beautifully captures the spirit of this expressionist artist. Her poetic text marries image and word in a satisfying tour de force.

Mayhew, James. *Katie Meets the Impressionists.* Orchard, 1997.
  In this, the first of several Katie adventures, a little girl visits the art museum with her grandma. Katie wanders away from Grandma and steps into Monet's painting of the luncheon. She picks flowers from Monet's garden, and then steps into another painting, one by Renoir of a little girl and her watering can. Later Katie joins Monet's son as he walks through a field of poppies with his mother. In the end, Katie dances on stage with Degas's dancers and accepts a bouquet of flowers, which she gives to Grandma back in the museum.

Mayhew, James. *Katie and the Mona Lisa.* Orchard, 1999.

Katie visits the art museum with her grandma. When she wishes she knew what makes the Mona Lisa smile, she is invited into the painting. Together the little girl and Mona Lisa visit other paintings in the museum and are able to enter the world of Saint George, get to know the dancers in Botticelli's *Primavera,* and have a close encounter with the lions of Venice. Katie returns to her own world just as her grandma awakens from a nap, unaware of Katie's adventure.

Mayhew, James. *Katie and the Sunflowers.* Orchard, 2000.

Katie returns to the art museum with her grandma. This time she upsets the vase of sunflowers in a Van Gogh painting, joins the Breton girls in a work by Gauguin, leaps into Van Gogh's night cafe, spills some of Cezanne's apples, and travels to Tahiti via another Gauguin masterpiece. Everything is set aright as Grandma wakes up, knowing nothing of Katie's latest adventure.

Rubin, Susan Goldman. *The Yellow House.* Illus. Jos. A. Smith. Abrams/The Art Institute of Chicago, 2001.

This introduction to Van Gogh's life in the south of France in the famous yellow house with Gauguin recaptures the lively world of these two artists and their works. Compare Van Gogh's portrait of Madame Ginoux with Gauguin's work showing the same woman in a night scene of a smoky cafe. Smith's passion-filled paintings of the two artists bring this tumultuous period to life for young readers.

Visconti, Guido. *The Genius of Leonardo.* Illus. Bimba Landmann. Barefoot Books, 2000.

Learn about Leonardo's life and works through the eyes of his young apprentice. Landmann's distinctive illustrations rendered in Byzantine style from an earlier age will cause students to look at the world in a new way.

Waldman, Neil. *The Starry Night.* Boyds Mills Press, 1999.

Told through the eyes of a modern-day boy in New York City, this unique story imagines what would happen if Vincent were alive in our own time and painted scenes of the American city. Waldman's paintings of such places as the Statue of Liberty, Brooklyn Bridge, and Times Square are painted as Van Gogh would have painted them. The last painting the boy sees is Vincent's glorious "Starry Night." Children will be excited to see other children's renditions of this painting filling the endpapers of the book.

Winter, Jeannette. *Diego.* Illus. Jonah Winter. Knopf, 1991.

In a bilingual text, this mother and son team tells us about the life and works of the famous Mexican muralist, Diego Rivera. Winter's folk-art style, featured in little frames, is well matched with the brief but illuminating text.

Winter, Jeannette. *My Name Is Georgia: A Portrait.* Silver Whistle, 1998.

Similar in format and style to the book, *Diego,* young artists will linger over the scenes from New Mexico that inspired many of O'Keefe's paintings.

Winter, Jonah. *Frida.* Illus. Ana Juan. Arthur Levine/Scholastic, 2002.

The fantasy and pain of Frida Kahlo's life is beautifully told through folk art and sparse text. The feeling is both dreamlike and slightly grotesque. In one especially remarkable two-page spread, silhouettes of birds float across the page with one transforming into Kahlo's distinctively heavy brows. This should inspire children to stretch their imagination through word and picture.

Art Activities

Your Very Own Art Museum

In this activity, children will research the art books in the library, select favorite works of art, and then set up their own art museum. They also learn to be art critics when they choose the art they prefer and explain their reason for making their selections.

Materials Needed

1. Art books from the library collection

2. Postcard or poster-sized art reproductions

3. Posterboard to mount artworks

4. Posterboard or construction paper to make signs

5. Ribbons in bright colors to hold pages open in art books

6. Markers, scissors, and glue for sign making

Procedure

1. Plan an "art walk" through books about art and artists in your library, or select a variety of art books and arrange them in a display or on a book cart for children to review.

2. Gather postcards or posters of artworks. Browse the Internet to find reproductions of artworks. Use Web sites from museums such as the Metropolitan Museum of Art in New York (www.metmuseum.org), the Louvre in Paris (www.louvre.fr/louvrea.htm), the Van Gogh Museum in Amsterdam (www.vangoghmuseum.nl).

3. Ask students to choose their favorite works of art and begin a museum of their own. Children select postcards, posters, or books with art reproductions to display on a table or in a corner of the library.

4. Children may mount the posters or postcards on posterboard. Provide ribbons to tie around open pages in art books.

5. Give children extra paper and markers to name their museum. Typical examples might be "John's Museum of Art," or "Amy's Modern Art Gallery," or "The Museum of Flowers and Gardens."

6. After everyone has organized their museum, encourage children to take the group on an "art walk" to individual galleries. Each person describes their art and explains why the different pieces were chosen.

Sunny Days and Starry Nights: A Van Gogh Celebration

For this program, set up activity stations so that children can choose their favorite Van Gogh project. In preparation, arrange bouquets of real, silk, or paper sunflowers on bookcases and hang large cardboard stars from the ceiling. Make copies of the artists' chairs (Fig. 2.1) for participants. Display books about Van Gogh and his paintings on tables around the room.

Materials Needed

1. Real, silk, or paper sunflowers (purchased from discount craft stores)

2. Yellow cardboard for stars

3. Shoeboxes for yellow houses

4. Photocopies of artist chairs illustrated in this chapter (Fig. 2.1)

5. Colored markers, pencils, and watercolors

6. White art paper, yellow construction paper, green cardboard

7. White paper plates

8. Yellow paint

9. Sunflower seeds

10. Craft sticks

11. Reproductions of Van Gogh paintings printed from the Van Gogh Web site (www.vangoghmuseum.nl)

12. Van Gogh books from your collection (Neil Waldman's *The Starry Night,* Susan Rubin Goldman's book *The Yellow House,* and Bob Hersey's *Van Gogh's House: A Pop-Up Experience,* and those listed in the bibliography of this chapter)

13. Audio music recording for mood music and an audio player (e.g., cassette or CD player)

Procedure

1. Set up the Sunflower Show Station with paper plates, paint, sunflower seeds, pictures of sunflowers cut out from magazines or printed from a Web site (use www.google.com to search the Internet), and yellow and green paper.

2. *Sunflower Project One:* Cut around the edge of a paper plate to make petals of flower, but leave enough of the plate intact in the middle to glue sunflower seeds for the center. This creates a realistic and textured flower center. Glue flower on a green cardboard stem or on a craft stick if desired.

3. *Sunflower Project Two:* Glue pictures of sunflowers on yellow construction paper. Glue craft stick stems. "Plant" the sunflowers around the wall to create a sunflower garden. Poetic children may want to write sunflower poems to add to this display. Simply give children the beginning line "Sunflowers, on my mind . . ." and encourage them to complete the poem.

4. Set up the Starry Night Activity area with several copies of Neil Waldman's book *The Starry Night,* or read from your own copy and display a poster reproduction of Van Gogh's *Starry Night* painting. Read the book, then give children white art paper, markers, colored pencils, and paints to create their own starry night pictures. Play mood music to inspire children. A recording of Mussorgsky's "Pictures at an Exhibition" or Don McLean's "Vincent" are appropriate choices.

5. Set up a Yellow House activity area with copies of Susan Goldman Rubin's book *The Yellow House* and a copy of Bob Hersey's *Van Gogh's House: A Pop-Up Experience.* Provide each child with a shoebox and photocopies of the Van Gogh chairs shown in this chapter (Fig. 2.1). Children may cover the boxes with yellow construction paper or paint the outside with yellow paint. Older children may wish to add details such as windows and a colored roof. Inside the house children may glue the chairs, adding little stands so the chairs will stand up. Color reproductions of Van Gogh's paintings from the Van Gogh Museum Web site can be glued to the inside walls of the house for decoration. Older children may wish to draw their own chairs instead of using the photocopies provided.

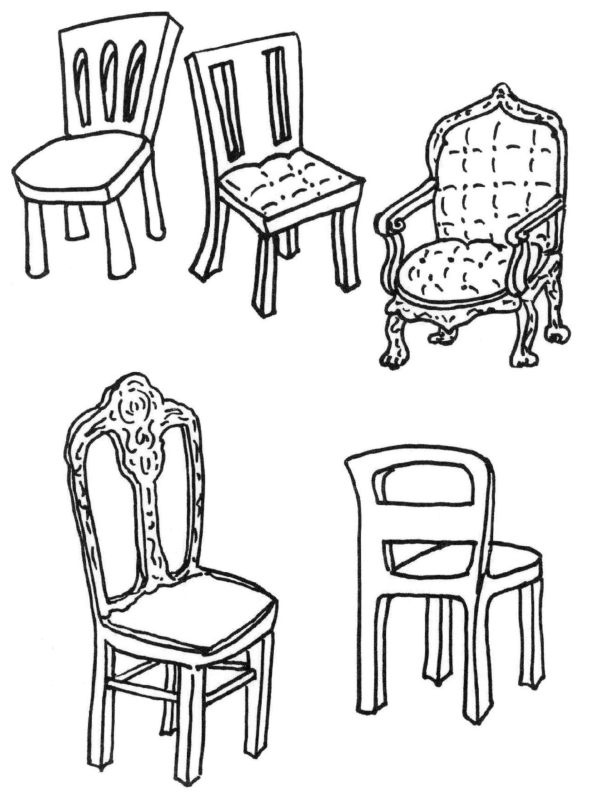

Figure 2.1

Cut-Up Capers: A Matisse Celebration

Although Matisse painted many scenes and portraits, near the end of his life, he made collages of shapes. These were arranged in compositions with titles such as *The Snail, The Sheaf,* and a series of works called *Jazz.* In these activities, children will become familiar with shapes and make their own projects to take home. Note that the beginning activities of reading and dancing will appeal to children strong in verbal-linguistic intelligence and those gifted with bodily-kinesthetic intelligence.

In preparation, make photocopy patterns of Matisse shapes (Fig. 2.2) in different sizes, and have volunteers bake cookies shaped in these patterns.

Materials Needed

1. Colored construction paper or colored card stock

2. Long pieces of posterboard or mat board

3. Wire clothes hangers

4. Colored yarn

5. Snacks, if desired (see the following procedures)

6. A copy of Le Tord's *A Bird or Two*

7. Audio recording and audio player for mood music

Procedure

1. Set up two project areas and a story corner. Assemble children first in the story corner.

2. Read Le Tord's book *A Bird or Two* to the entire group. Using some of the books in this chapter's bibliography, provide details about Matisse's life. Ask children to use words or phrases that come to mind as they are shown reproductions of Matisse's art. Dance students could be invited to wear brightly colored tights and compose a freestyle dance as they undulate colored scarves. After this introduction, guide children to the project tables.

3. At the collage table, provide children with patterns based on the illustrations in Figure 2.2. Instruct them to cut out construction paper shapes either using the patterns or creating shapes of their own. Arrange these in random order, or create a composition in the style of Matisse. If you wish, suggest titles for their compositions, such as *Life Under the Sea, Spring Garden,* or *Dance in Space.* As children create their collage works, play compositions such as "Round Midnight" or "Wild Man Blues" played by Miles Davis, or Duke Ellington's "Mood Indigo" or "Perdido." Display the collages with children's titles, or mount the collages on pieces of posterboard to take home.

4. At the mobile and display table, provide children with coat hangers and Matisse shapes cut on mat board (based on Fig. 2.2). Guide them in punching holes in the shapes and tying them to the coat hangers with yarn to make mobiles. Suggest that the yarn might be cut in various lengths so the mobiles will display shapes at various levels. (Asymmetrical designs are pleasing to the eye.) Other children may wish to tie their shapes to tree boughs or evergreen branches. You may wish to attach other shapes to ribbons suspended from doorways so that children and parents will literally enter the world of a work by Matisse.

5. As a finale, serve children cookies cut into Matisse shapes from sugar cookie dough. (Volunteers can make the cookies ahead, or teen cooks participating in other library programs may be willing to supply the treats.)

Figure 2.2

Idea Springboards: Activities to Develop

Georgia on My Mind

After reading *My Name Is Georgia,* ask children to discuss how Georgia O'Keefe forced us to look at details in objects that we might not have seen before. Give children real flowers to observe. Look at close-up photographs of flowers. Show the children the illustrations in this chapter (Figs. 2.3–2.5). Then provide children with colored pencils and art paper to make their own flower pictures. Some children may want to make flower triptychs with three views of the same flower: a shot of the flower showing just its center, a middle view that shows the center and half of the petals, and a full-sized flower showing its details.

Grant Wood's American Gothic

Grant Wood's famous painting of a farmer and his wife standing in front of a Gothic-style barn has become a symbol of an American farm scene. Provide farm clothes for children to wear as they pose in front of various scenes projected on a wall. You can use slides of famous sites such as the Statue of Liberty or a McDonald's arch. Children may take different poses than the stiff postures of the American Gothic couple. Student artists may wish to draw these variations on a theme, and student writers can compose news stories about "Farmer and Mrs. Wood Travel America."

Frida's Dream

Read Winter's book *Frida* to your students. This book focuses on the painful sequences of the artist's life with dreamlike images. Encourage students to describe dreams and discuss how the artist might have been inspired in her work because of the physical pain she endured. Have children do self-portraits of themselves surrounded by dream images or pictures inspired by their own dreams. As an alternative project, simply focus on making dream paintings or collages on themes such as "Nightmare Number One," "Fantasy Dreamland," or "Carried Away by My Dreams."

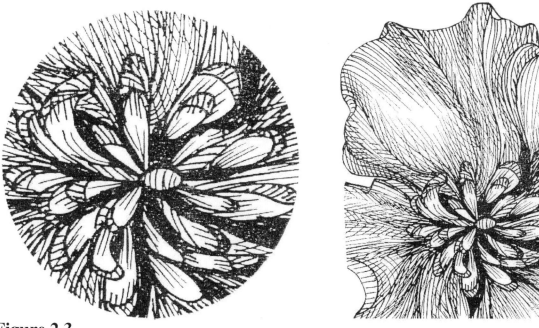

Figure 2.3

Figure 2.4

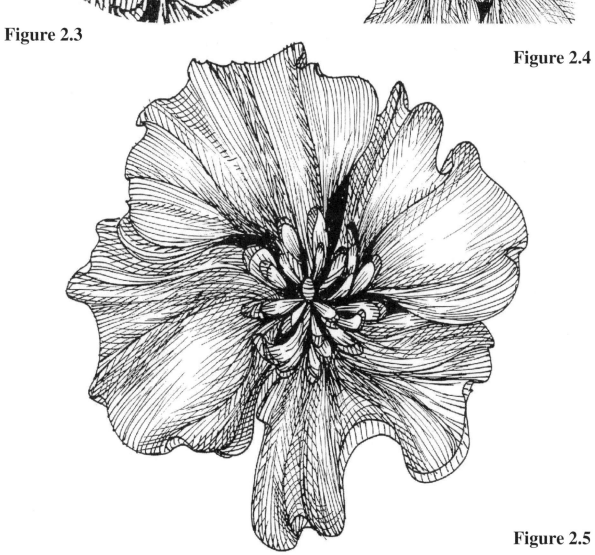

Figure 2.5

3

Count Down

Books and Activities about Math

Before children enter school, most learn to count up to ten, recite their house number, and see prices on grocery store items. They will hold up five fingers to show you how old they are, memorize their telephone numbers, and tell you the date of their birthdays. They may know the rhyme "Ten Bears in the Bed" in which one bear at a time falls out of bed with none left in the end. These children understand adding and subtracting. When children can tell you a triangle has three sides and a square has four sides, they know basic geometry.

We use math quite naturally every day. Children can learn numbers by playing cards with a grandparent or measuring one cup of flour in the kitchen. They understand the concepts of "more" or "less" by counting out their allowance and spending their own money.

Yet even with all this real-word experience, the subject of math in school can excite or frighten children. Today the phrase "math anxiety" describes those negative feelings large numbers of children and adults associate with the topic. Those of us raised before calculators became little adding machines and multiplication chanters. We satisfied math requirements to graduate from high school and college, but did we grow in math confidence? Did we discover the joy of thinking mathematically? Sadly, too many of us shied away from anything to do with the dreaded "M" word, and we were diminished because of this fear.

Many school children with dyslexia become discouraged when they are not allowed to use these tools to help them move on to math functions that could encourage them to participate in real "math thinking."

Children without these limitations still need to connect math in the real world along with math activities that integrate art, social studies, science, or even physical education. Not everyone is gifted with math-logic intelligence, but we all can grow in appreciation and understanding of these principles. Rosemary Wells tells us in the author's note to *Emily's First 100 Days of School* that she, as a child, did not think math was fun because it was taught by rote. Marilyn Kaye's *A Day with No Math* strikes a responsive chord for children who identify with the main character who doesn't want to do his math homework, then declares he wishes there was "no such thing as math."

Fortunately, there are an increasing number of books that explore math thinking by appealing to children's natural curiosity. Vickie Krudwig's *Cucumber Soup* tells the reader fascinating facts about insects, teaching counting, and combines this with a great story. Kids learn about math through Amy Axelrod's clever books set in restaurants, kitchens, and at the beach. Humorous stories place math in our everyday world, allowing children to have so much fun that they forget they are learning. Other books listed in this chapter's bibliography feature math riddles, a math-measuring kid who wins a big contest, and a math superman who performs great feats in a superstore. At last, math has entered the world of children's literature where we can scratch our heads, laugh, and be inspired to make up our own stories.

Books about Math and Literature

Axelrod, Amy. *Pigs Will Be Pigs*. Simon & Schuster, 1994.

This is the first Pig family storybook with a math slant features. Mr. and Mrs. Pig and the children experience zany adventures while learning math. The family decides to go out for dinner at the Enchanted Enchilada. They search the house for loose change, a few dollar bills, and then are on their way. The full-sized menu shown in the book allows children to make their choices while the Pig family selects theirs. At the end, the author's note asks children questions about choosing other items on the menu to spend money wisely.

Other titles about the Pig family by the same author: *Pigs in the Pantry: Fun with Math and Cooking* and *Pigs on a Blanket: Fun with Math and Time*.

Clement, Rod. *Counting on Frank*. Gareth Stevens, 1991.

A father tells his math whiz-kid son, "You have a brain. Use it!" The curious kid calculates how many Franks (his dog) will fit into his bedroom, how long it would take for the bathroom to fill with water if he left the water running, and how many peas it would take to fill up the kitchen. The kid wins a jelly-bean guessing contest that gives him a trip to Hawaii. Clement's clever story presents young readers with more math puzzles at the end of the book.

Daniels, Teri. *Math Man*. Orchard/Scholastic, 2001.

Mrs. Gourd takes her class to Mighty Mart, a super store, so that they can see math in action. Mr. Budget, the manager greets them, but Garth, the stock boy, is the character who really puts on a show. Garth bags groceries, juggles potatoes, and shows the class how to buy the right quantities for a family of five. When the super scanners break down, the cashiers can't add up the orders. Fortunately, Garth has a way with numbers, and, to the relief of all, he adds up all the grocery items in everyone's cart.

Kaye, Marilyn. *A Day with No Math*. Harcourt Brace Jovanovich, 1992.

Sam dislikes math and avoids his math homework. As he falls asleep one night, he makes a wish that there was no such thing as math. In his dream, he goes through a day without clocks, rulers, sports with no way to score, and dozens of other dilemmas—all because there is no math in the world. Fortunately, it was all a dream.

Krudwig, Vickie Lee. *Cucumber Soup*. Fulcrum, 1998.

In this humorous picture book about counting, insects of all kinds and numbers munch their way into a giant cucumber. Sidebars provide insect lore, and the book ends with a fun activity—make a cold cucumber soup or a cucumber dip for children to enjoy—the recipes are included!

Munsch, Robert. *Moira's Birthday*. Annick Press, 1987.

Munsch's humorous storytelling skills relate the outlandish story of Moira, who invites every kid in school to her birthday party. When everyone arrives, Moira has to order enough pizza and birthday cakes for the crowd. Her wild estimates and the crazy results of her bulk buys provide fun for readers, who can then make up their own estimating and planning games for class parties.

Nagda, Ann Whitehead, and Cindy Bickel. *Tiger Math and Learning to Graph from a Baby Tiger*. Henry Holt, 2000.

Based on actual events, this engaging book tells the story of T. J., a Siberian tiger cub born at the Denver Zoo. When the cub stops eating one day, the zoo staff begin a program to tempt the animal to begin eating again. The book traces her weight with charts that will capture the attention of animal lovers, who learn math as the story progresses.

Neuschwander, Cindy. *Sir Cumference and the First Round Table.* Charlesbridge, 1997.

King Arthur, tired of trying to shout to his knights because they are seated at a long table, enlists the help of his wife and the knight Sir Cumference to solve this math problem. They explore all kinds of shapes for the king's table, from parallelograms to ovals to octagons, before they settle on a round table. Children will love the problem-solving ideas and will want to create their own shape stories.

Scieszka, Jon, and Lane Smith. *Math Curse.* Penguin, 1995.

Mrs. Fibonacci tells her class that they can think of almost everything as a math problem. One student begins having problems the next day. He worries about the number of clothes in his closet, how long it will take him to brush his teeth, and how the food will be distributed at lunch. Every subject seems to contain math problems. In geography class, he wonders how many M&Ms it would take to measure the Mississippi River. In time, he becomes a math lunatic—until he breaks the math curse.

Slote, Joseph. *Miss Bindergarten Celebrates the 100th Day of Kindergarten.* Dutton, 1998.

Miss Bindergarten instructs her students to bring "100 of some wonderful, one-hundred-full things" to school the next day. The animal "children" bring paper chains, blocks, candy hearts, crafts they have made, and more. The delightful teacher does 100 sit-ups and serves punch with 100 cherries. This is a great book for teachers to celebrate the concept of 100 and inspire children to think about making their own 100 collections.

Tang, Greg. *The Grapes of Math.* Illus Harry Briggs. Scholastic Press, 2001.

Tang's fascinating poems combine with bright illustrations to challenge young readers to solve various problems: counting grapes on a vine, cherries by the bunch, and empty prairie dog holes. Answers with explanations appear at the end.

Math Activities

Party Time! A Week of Math and Fun

Who wouldn't want to party every day of the week? Combine math activities with these festive math activities, which are guaranteed to turn frowns into smiles. In public libraries, choose your favorite activities for one big party afternoon. The activities can be conducted over a week or in weekly sessions over five weeks.

Materials Needed

1. Tables for children to display their math collections

2. A hot plate, an electric wok, and basic kitchen utensils

3. Ingredients for several recipes, such as canned chicken broth and dry noodles, cheese and crackers, cooked rice, a dozen eggs, soy sauce, chopped onion

4. Purchased food, such as pizzas, banana bread, small chocolate candies in individual bags, cole slaw

5. Colored paper and markers to make menus

6. Lined 3-by-5-inch index cards

7.   Copies of Joseph Slote's *Miss Bindergarten Celebrates the 100th Day of Kindergarten* and of Amy Axelrod's *Pigs in the Pantry*.

8.   A camera to take pictures of your celebration.

Procedure

The day before you begin this week of activities (Friday before the following Monday will give children a weekend to gather their items), read aloud *Miss Bindergarten Celebrates the 100th Day of Kindergarten*. If children are in Grades 1 or 2, you might rename the book "Miss Gade Celebrates the 100th Day of First Grade" or "Miss Wade Celebrates the 100th Day of Second Grade" and reword the text accordingly. Brainstorm with the children the different kinds of collections or objects they can bring to celebrate Party Day One. Each child brings in 100 items or shares a game or activity with 100 parts. (See ideas below.)

Day One

1.   Reread the book if desired.

2.   Provide tables for children to display their collections.

3.   Ask children to show and tell about their collections. Note that the idea lists that follow suggest various kinds of objects, as well as actions for children who prefer physical activity or who have music or drama skills.

4.   Collections Idea List: buttons, pennies, greeting cards, marbles, individually wrapped candies, beads to string, popcorn kernels, stickers, strips of colored paper, playing cards, adhesive stars.

5.   Physical Activity Idea List: Ask children who are athletically inclined to bring in a basketball, a beach ball, or a jump rope and to come prepared to do 100 actions with the item, such as bouncing the ball 100 times or jumping rope 100 jumps.

6.   Musical or Dramatic Idea List: Suggest that children plan an activity with 100 actions involved. A starter list could include the following: sing 100 notes. Teach the class "100 Bottles of Milk in the Fridge" (substituting the line "Take one out, pass it around, 100 bottles of milk in the fridge" for "100 bottles of beer on the wall"). Teach the class 100 kinds of facial expressions or ways to move across a stage. Perhaps some kids will be able to recite or read 100 lines of poetry!

7.   Take plenty of photographs to remember the day. After displaying them for the week, you can give copies to children to take home.

8.   An alternative to this activity is to invite children to bring in as many kinds of printed materials as they can find to show how vital reading and math are in our lives. Suggestions include bus schedules, recipes, movie tickets, newspaper ads, labels from cans, bills, sports scores, play programs, game cards, a cereal box, and so on. Have plenty of items of your own so the final total will add up to 100. Tape these to the floor in the library with clear cellophane tape as a visual reminder of the importance of reading and math.

Day Two

1.   Read *Pigs in the Pantry* to the children.

2.   Instruct children to find the cookbook section of the library, or select simple cookbooks for children and put them on display. Have children choose a cookbook and copy three recipes on index cards you have given them.

3.   Invite children to make up funny names for their recipes, related to the names of book characters they know.

4. You can have children bring food items to your next meeting; or if you have cooking facilities, you can have them bring ingredients and cook a dish together. You could choose to do both as well. Ask children to make a dish at home from the cookbook and bring it on Day Three, or have them choose a picture book about food for your own recipe planning, and assign each child one ingredient to bring to the next meeting.

5. Idea List of books and recipe starters:

> *Curious George*—banana bread (purchased or made from mix)
>
> *Big Cheese for the White House*—cheese and crackers
>
> *A Pizza the Size of the Sun* or *Moira's Birthday*—several pizzas
>
> *Everybody Cooks Rice*—ingredients for Chinese stir-fried rice
>
> *Charlie and the Chocolate Factory*—purchased bag of individually wrapped chocolate candy
>
> *Everybody Eats Soup*—basic ingredients for chicken noodle soup or several cans of soup
>
> *Little Red Hen*—purchased whole-wheat bread
>
> *Strega Nona*—cans of spaghetti or dry spaghetti and purchased spaghetti sauce
>
> *The Tortilla Factory* or *Big Moon Tortilla*—taco chips
>
> *There's a Cow in the Cabbage Patch*—purchased cabbage or cole slaw

Day Three

1. Sample the food everyone brings or make a few of the dishes with the class such as Chinese fried rice, chicken noodle soup, spaghetti.

2. Take advantage of measuring, counting, and estimating as you proceed.

3. Read one or more of the books listed in the Day Two idea list.

Day Four

1. Create your own wacky restaurant in the spirit of "The Enchanted Enchilada" (in *Pigs Will Be Pigs*) by giving children construction paper and markers to make their own menus.

2. Do this activity in the library and encourage children to name the food items for characters in Mother Goose collections or famous book characters.

3. If the classroom or library has enough computers, these menus can be made using a computer program. Here is a sample menu:

Mother Goose's Tea Room

Located at the Corner of Drury Lane and Farmer MacGregor's Organic Food Store for Your Convenience

Little Red Hen Basket of Tea Rolls $2.00

Muffin Man's Blueberry Muffin $1.25

Chicken Licken's Scrambled Egg Plate $2.50

Glass of Cow That Jumped Over the Moon Milk $1.00

Peter Rabbit's Organic Tea $1.50

Jack Sprat's No Fat Cereal $1.25

Queen of Hearts Strawberry Tart $2.00

Delicious Treats for Our Bookish Friends!

---

4. Instruct children to bring in a menu from their favorite restaurant for the next day, or bring in an assortment of menus you have collected.

Day Five

1. Collect the menus children have brought in. You should have a variety of restaurant types—ethnic, fast food, family restaurants, or specialty places such as bagel shops or salad and soup places.

2. Give each child a menu and a play $20 bill to spend as they order a meal for four people. You can have children write a list with prices, if you like.

3. Then give each child a play $10 bill to spend on three people. This time they will have to make more economical choices.

Playing with Math Stories

In preparation, choose any literature stories that involve food and counting to act out. The selections I use as examples here are *Cucumber Soup* and *Pigs Will Be Pigs*.

Materials Needed

1. Copies of the selected books (e.g., Vickie Lee Krudwig's *Cucumber Soup* and Amy Axelrod's *Pigs Will Be Pigs*)

2. Photocopies of the insects shown in this chapter (Fig. 3.1)

3. Colored pencils to color the insects

4. Craft sticks to mount the insects for stick puppets

5. Long English cucumbers (these are longer than other cucumbers), two to four, depending on the size of the group.

6. Basic costumes for the pig family such as a beanie for the boy pig, a string of beads for the girl pig, glasses for father pig, and a purse and head scarf for mother pig.

7. Paper and pens or a word processing program for writing the pig script

Procedure **(Cucumber Soup** *Activity)*

Children love stories about large quantities of food, and this story fills the bill quite well. You can read aloud from the book or use storytelling. To tell the complete story, choose a few children to read the sidebar information in the book about each insect. Instruct other children to come to the front of the room as the story is told to stick insects into the cucumber as the story progresses.

1. Color and cut out the photocopied insects (Fig. 3.1) and tape each to a craft stick. Make one copy of each kind of bug. If you want to count out all the various numbers of insects, you will need to make many photocopies and purchase several cucumbers so there is room for all the insects to be stuck in the cucumber(s).

2. Read the story to the children first.

3. Setting one cucumber aside, reread or retell the story with children reading the sidebars orally and sticking the insects in the cucumber(s).

4. Roll the cucumber(s) over at the end of the story.

5. Make the cucumber soup or dip from the recipe given at the end of the story, with children reading, measuring, and making it.

Procedure **(Pigs Will Be Pigs** *Readers Theatre Play)*

1. Dress the pig characters, using suggestions from the materials listed earlier, or use your own ideas.

2. Turn the Axelrod book into a readers' theatre script. Even if you haven't done this before, it's easy. Have one or two children read aloud the words in the book, except for the direct quotes of the pig family. Assign the actual pig quotes to the four pigs. Remember there are also parts for the waitress and waiters at the restaurant.

3. Type out the scripts and practice reading the parts aloud until the children are able to read the story smoothly.

4. Invite another class to watch the story reenacted.

5. Give everyone a copy of the menu and ask them to make their own selections, spending no more than $34.67, as in the story. *Note:* Instruct the children that no one can choose the specials and to think carefully so they don't overspend their money. Remind them to save enough for a 10-percent tip.

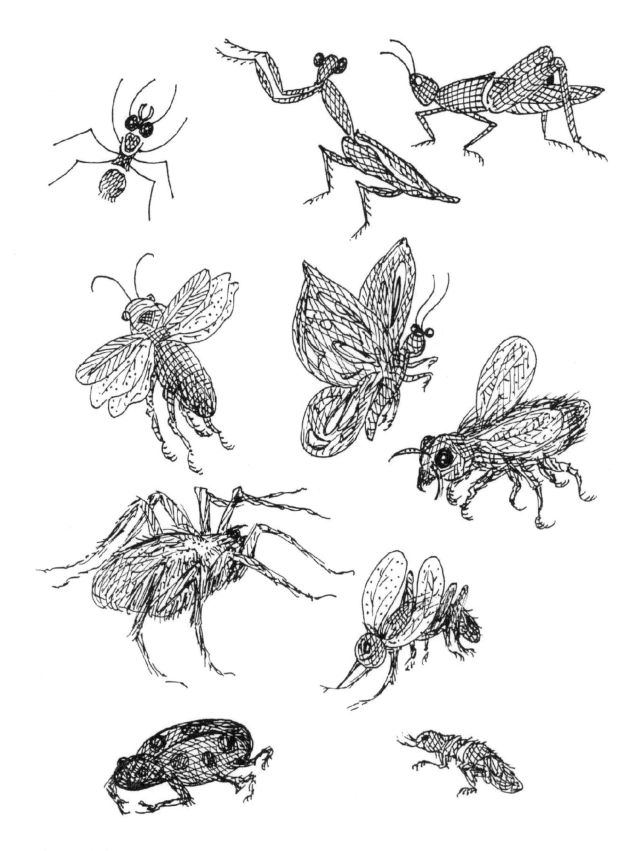

Figure 3.1

Idea Springboards: Activities to Develop

Math Pictures and Patterns

Greg Tang's books teach children to perform math functions by visualizing patterns of objects and details of objects. Choose a theme such as "Math Around the House" or "Vacation Math." Have children draw three pictures with objects to show math patterns. Examples might be patterns on a wallpapered wall, tiles on a bathroom wall, umbrellas on the beach, objects in a picnic basket.

As an alternative activity, use actual objects; for example, arrange cookies in different patterns on a cookie sheet or line up spoons on a large tray. Arrange and rearrange the objects to teach various math concepts.

Grocery Carts

Have children practice to become a Super Math Man or Woman inspired by the book *Math Man*.

Fill the cart with numerous food items (or pictures of food items cut from old magazines), each marked with the price. Have children practice adding up the cost of the items. Remove items from the grocery cart to about ten, and round off the prices. Now ask children to do the addition in their heads.

The Estimating Game

Using the following exercise, teach children how to estimate the amount of time a given task will take. Choose simple, familiar tasks for the children, such as reading the page of a book, doing pushups, or writing a paragraph about what they had for breakfast or the steps in making a bed. Ask the children to work with a partner and estimate how long each task will take. Then have children do the task as the partners time and see how accurate their estimates were. This activity teaches task completion and estimating skills; it also helps children become aware of time itself.

Crazy Day Math

Turn math curses into ways to "catch the math bug." Challenge children to solve the following math problems and make up their own math activities to stump the class. Use this list as a springboard.

1. Make up three math questions about getting to school on time.

2. Take an inventory of the items in your closet. Count sets of clothes by type: shirts, shoes, sweaters, and so on. Make a chart to show each category.

3. Make up lunch problems. If you have twenty kids in your room, how many sandwich halves will you have to make to give each kid one and a half sandwiches? Divide apples into quarters so each person will receive a quarter. Divide a 9-by-13-inch pan of brownies into equal-sized pieces so that everyone will get one.

4. Create three math problems based on the game of baseball.

5. Estimate the number of books on a library shelf. Count the books. Estimate the books on another shelf. Count them. Now count the number of shelves in the library and estimate how many books are in the collection. This could be a group project.

6. Assume you have to catch the school bus by 7:00 A.M. Write down everything you have to do before you get to the bus, including the time it takes to walk to the bus stop. Now allot time for each activity. Did you complete all the tasks in time? Try this out on a Friday or Saturday so that students will catch the bus on time the following Monday.

7. What time should people go to bed if they have to set the alarm for 6:00, 6:15, or 6:30 A.M. and need eight hours of sleep?

8. Tell students to make a budget based on a weekly allowance of $8. Their parents tell them to save half of the money. How much will they spend on each of the following items: tickets to a movie (or renting a video or DVD), snacks to enjoy while watching the movie, a small present for their best friend, and a school supply such as a notebook? Did they have any money left?

A Penny Saved Is a Penny Earned

Ben Franklin's simple statement "A penny saved is a penny earned" is more complicated if you invest your money. Assume you save a dime a day, and your father tells you he will give you a dime for every dime you save. In a week, how much money will you have? In a 30-day month, how much money will you have? In one year (365 days), how much money will you have?

More advanced students could learn about investing money in the bank. At the end of one week, collect and count each child's money to invest in a bank. Now track what happens to the money at a 1.5-percent interest rate. This exercise could be simply an exercise in what would happen, or you can start a real investment in a class bank.

At the end of the savings period, students vote on a class activity that they would like to enjoy from the money they have made.

Math Guests

Invite several guests to the classroom or library to talk about how they use math in their jobs. Guests might include a sports writer, a chef, a bookkeeper, an investor, or a retail salesperson. Ask children to write out questions for the guests before the visit.

Each guest speaks for five to ten minutes about how math is important in his or her job. Kids ask their prepared questions.

The next day, ask children to discuss what they learned about the careers and the use of math in the real world.

Starring the Chef

Invite a local chef to do a food demonstration, or dress up as Julia Adult or Emeril Pepper Mill. Dress up with an apron or a chef's hat, or dress up in something wild. You could wear all red and appear as Chile Pepper Corey, or wear a wig and sunglasses and play Rhonda the Cooking Rock Star. Bring ingredients to make a crazy creation. As you prepare the dish, slowly announce the name of the ingredients and the amounts you are using.

Instruct children to write down the recipe, listing ingredients and amounts and recording the procedure. This encourages students to listen, to write down amounts carefully, and to record a sequence of steps.

Have children cut the recipe in half for a small family.

Final Suggestions

Take plenty of photographs of these math activities and exercises. Make posters or bulletin boards to motivate children to see everything in the world as a potential math problem.

Focus on the concept of estimating things. Every week set up a jar of something or a display of items to encourage estimating and thinking mathematically. You could use the sports page, newspaper ads, coupons, new menus—anything that involves numbers.

4

Food Feast

Programs and Books about Food

Why have so many stories and books been written on the topic of food? Is it because some people struggled to find enough food to eat and made up stories to satisfy their hunger? Is it because people have always been fascinated by food and eager to try something new? Is it true that "we are what we eat"? Is food simply basic to life? In my opinion, the answers are yes, yes, yes, and yes.

Robin Currie and I wrote two popular source books on food, *Mudluscious* (1986) and *Second Helpings* (1994). We easily found more than one hundred new books on the subject of food to fill each book. Old favorites from the "Gingerbread Boy" and the "Little Red Hen" to modern classics such as *Blueberries for Sal* and *Chicken Soup with Rice* were joined by the popular titles *Cloudy with a Chance for Meatballs* and *Growing Vegetable Soup*.

In recent years, more stories about international foods have been published as a result of growing multicultural awareness. Some of the books on international food topics published about twenty years ago included *How My Parents Learned to Eat* and the *Funny Little Woman*. There weren't many. Less than ten years later, several dozen followed. Some of my favorites have been *The Sleeping Bread*, set in Guatemala; *Rechenka's Eggs*, set in the Ukraine; and *Too Many Tamales*, featuring a Hispanic family in the United States. Newer titles include *Dim Sum for Everyone*, *Big Moon Tortilla*, and *A Mountain of Blintzes*. Note that all of these titles are books about food from many countries. We can travel the world through stories about food and then cook up ethnic dishes to help children broaden their appetites.

Common themes on this ever-fascinating topic employ word play of food terms found in *Fed Up*, and logical sequencing found in Laura Numeroff's titles *If You Give a Pig a Pancake*, *If You Give a Mouse a Cookie*, and *If You Give a Moose a Muffin*. Other food themes involve cooking huge quantities of food as in *Strega Nona*, arguing over who makes the best of something found in *Matzah Ball Soup*, and food that runs away found in many versions of *The Gingerbread Boy* and *The Runaway Tortilla*. Enjoying holiday foods in a family setting is a natural topic. In Gary Soto's *Too Many Tamales*, a Hispanic family makes tamales every year during the Christmas season. *The Matzah Man*, a new book by Naomi Howland, retells the Gingerbread Man tale as a matzah baker shapes his leftover dough into a man who runs throughout the neighborhood before he is eaten at a Passover meal.

Food topics are so popular with children that any program or activity you plan is likely to be a huge success. Favorite programs that I have participated in or planned include one in which a priest brought his pasta machine to make spaghetti for a hungry crowd of kids and another, a preschool story series, that combined making chicken soup with rice, serving bread and butter after reading Paul Galdone's *Little Red Hen*, and passing out blueberries after reading *Blueberries for Sal*. At a Chinese New Year party, children sniffed exotic spices and practiced using chopsticks. Finally, a Paul Bunyan party ended with us making a "Paul-sized" submarine sandwich.

Wonderful food stories continue to be published every year, and every family has a food story to share. Encourage children to tell their own food stories based on family events. Whatever your nationality or food interest, may everyone join in the spirit of this topic with a hearty appetite—in the words of the Italians, *Mangia!*

Books about Food

Cowley, Joy. *Big Moon Tortilla*. Boyds Mills, 1998.
> Maria ruins her homework, but Grandmother soothes her with an old story about healing and makes her a tortilla. Food forms a healing bond between them.

Doley, Norah. *Everybody Bakes Bread*. Carolrhoda, 1996.
> As a sequel to *Everybody Cooks Rice,* this book sends a young girl off to find an unusual cooking utensil; in the process, she collects bread recipes from around the world.

Donnelly, Jennifer. *Humble Pie*. Atheneum, 2002.
> Theo's grandmother seems to be the only one in the family who recognizes that the boy is spoiled rotten. At the height of his greed, Grandmother makes him a huge fruit pie that she calls "humble pie," which engulfs the greedy young eater. In the end Theo, is humbled into developing a sweet disposition.

Enderle, Judith Ross, and Stephanie Jacob Gordon. *Something's Happening on Calabash Street.* Chronicle, 2000.
> On Calabash Street, the air is filled with the scents of Mrs. Puccini's bread, the Chambal's curry, and the Dakarari's yams. When the sky becomes rosy, Mama and her children make their favorite dish and parade down the street to where lanterns are lit and the Calabash Street Fair begins. This joy-filled celebration will encourage children to enjoy the recipes included and make up their own stories.

Geeslin, Campbell. *How Nanita Learned to Make Flan*. Atheneum, 1999.
> A little girl in a Mexican town makes her own slippers because her father the cobbler is too busy, but the shoes take her far away. Nanita is held as a slave in a rich man's house, where she has to work much like Cinderella but learns how to make a magic flan. At last the resourceful girl finds her way home, where she makes the flan to the delight of the whole village. A recipe for flan is included.

Goldin, Barbara Diamond. *A Mountain of Blintzes*. Illus. Ank McGrory. Harcourt, 2001.
> Mother and Father try to save money to buy ingredients for blintzes to celebrate Shavuot, but they outsmart one another. Fortunately, the children are resourceful enough to get the ingredients so that the family has a mountain of blintzes for the holiday.

Lin, Grace. *Dim Sum for Everyone*. Knopf, 2001.
> This simple story describes a child enjoying a dim sum meal with her family in a restaurant in Chinatown. The bold illustrations and endpapers with ingredients will provide basic information for primary-school-age children about eating this delightful type of Chinese food.

Numeroff, Laura. *If You Give a Pig a Pancake*. Illus. Felicia Bond. HarperCollins, 1998.
> One of Numeroff's several engaging books of logical sequences that begin by giving an animal some food. These books are perfect for teaching reasoning and serve as models for children to write stories of their own. Other titles by this author are *If Your Give a Mouse a Cookie* and *If You Give Your Moose a Muffin.*

Numeroff, Laura, and Barney Saltzberg. *Two for the Stew*. Simon & Schuster, 1996.

The cover and book illustrations suggest a star-studded Broadway musical. The story is a conversation between a young woman and a waiter. The woman has come to the restaurant with her poodle to enjoy a stew for two, but there is none to be had. The catchy verse and narrative twists will appeal to young readers, and the book inspires other activities about food shows and theatrical events.

Paulsen, Gary. *The Tortilla Factory*. Illus. Ruth Wright Paulsen. Harcourt Brace & Company, 1995.

Brief text and expressive oil paintings tell a story that begins with corn grown in the fields, moves to a factory where the corn is used to make tortillas, and concludes with the tortillas being used to make tasty treats in the kitchen. The growing cycle is an excellent sequence story for young children.

Pittman, Helena Clare. *Still-Life Stew*. Illus. Victoria Raymond. Hyperion, 1998.

Rosa grows many vegetables and picks them. Then she paints the food with bright colors and makes her own stew from the veggies. The book includes a recipe for the stew. The story is engaging, and the pictures of clay figures will intrigue children from a wide range of ages. Art, food, and story combine to make an unusual book.

Rosen, Michael J. *Food Fight*. Harcourt Brace & Company, 1998.

This collection of delicious poems from children's book authors will inspire young people to write food poems, and proceeds from the book help the international organization Share Our Strength in its efforts to eliminate world hunger.

Rothenberg, Joan. *Matzah Ball Soup*. Hyperion, 1999.

Rosie, a young girl, watches her aunts make their own versions of matzah ball soup as the family competes for the best recipe. Uncle Russell saves the day when he announces that every Seder meal must include a matzah ball made by each of the aunts.

Sayre, April Pulley. *Noodle Man*. Illustrated by Stephen Castanza. Orchard/Scholastic, 2002.

"Al Dente" invents a wonderful pasta machine but is unsuccessful in marketing it. Fortunately, the resourceful Mr. Dente finds that pasta is a very adaptable food with many other uses.

Steig, William. *Pete's a Pizza*. HarperCollins, 1998.

A feisty young boy who is bored enjoys his grandfather's play in turning the child into a human pizza. Younger elementary children will laugh at the antics.

Stevens, Janet, and Susan Stevens Crummel. *Cook-a-Doodle-Doo!* Illus. Janet Stevens. Harcourt Brace & Company, 1999.

Rooster invites his assistants, Turtle, Iguana, and Pot Bellied Pig, to make a wonderful strawberry shortcake, but none of his friends know how to cook. Rooster steps in to help. Humorous lines and funny mistakes keep the story lively from first to last.

Library Food Programs

The Public Library Setting: Dinner Theater

In a public library setting, you can stage a children's version of a dinner theater. Practice the following skits, stories, and songs with children before the event if you want to present it "performance style" for families. As narrator, greet the audience and provide introductions to the different activities described below.

The narrator can wear a sandwich board (described in Chapter 1) with a playbill announcing the dinner theater group, "The Peanut Butter Kids."

Materials Needed

1. A display of food books and cookbooks to check out

2. A sandwich board (as described in Chapter 1)

3. Posterboard and long dowels for the salad bar characters

4. Large photocopies of the salad bar illustrations in this chapter (Figs. 4.1–4.7) and posterboard on which to mount them, glue, craft sticks, and color markers or crayons

5. Cake boxes purchased from bakeries

6. Ribbon, ten or more yards, to tie cake boxes to children's heads

7. Large flat basket

8. Several packages of pita bread or brown wrapping paper (brown paper grocery bags also work)

9. Snack tray to serve as refreshments (suggestions: relish tray of carrots, olives, celery sticks with peanut butter, cherry tomatoes, green pepper strips, a large sheet cake)

10. Paper plates, napkins

11. Two or more cakes to give away for the cakewalk activity

Procedure

1. Make a sandwich board according to the directions in Chapter 1.

2. Color or have children color the large photocopies of the salad bar characters (Figs. 4.1–4.7) of this chapter and mount on posterboard and glue to craft sticks for children to hold.

3. Cut out ten circles of brown paper (ten inches each). Arrange one circle on top of another, stapling the edges of the circles together half way around. Then stuff crumpled paper between the two circles to give a puffy shape to the "fake" pita. Staple the rest of the circle around the edges.

4. Place pita bread in a flat basket with a sign reading "Bread for Sale" (or make paper pita bread for the basket).

5. Photocopy scripts (provided below) for children to practice their parts. The lines are brief, so the children should be able to learn the lines quickly.

6. Practice the dinner theater show once with scripts and, at least, two other times with props before the performance.

7.   On the night of the dinner theater performance, announce the show with the first activity, "The Peanut Butter Kids Chant."

8.   Follow this greeting with the narrator (or a storyteller) telling the interactive story "Bread for Sale" (see story script on p. 56) .This story may be practiced with the kids in your acting group. An alternative approach might have the storyteller pass out the pita bread to children in the audience so they may spontaneously become part of the story as it is told.

9.   Follow this story with kids performing the "Chorus of the Salad Bar" and the "Salad Bar Song."

10.   The Salad Bar kids invite the audience to make a huge circle around the room, join hands, and sing the chorus of the "Salad Bar Song."

11.   Have the children wearing cake boxes tied to their heads pass out numbers to the audience. (Note that you will need duplicate numbers because you will draw at least two numbers for two people to receive the prize cakes.) Announce to the audience that the next activity is a cakewalk.

12.   Two children or two small groups sing the songs. One group sings the angel food cake song, the other sings the devil's food cake song.

13.   After the songs are sung, play recorded music of "My Bonnie Lies over the Ocean" as the audience walks around the room in a large circle. Stop the music at an appropriate time. Draw a number from a cake box, and announce the number. The audience member holding the matching number wins the first cake. Repeat this song and action until the next cake or cakes are given away.

14.   To end your program, have the Peanut Butter Kids do their final good-bye chant.

15.   Have the players serve food snacks to the audience.

Note: I have not provided costume ideas for the children because several activities follow the performance. All players may wear white T-shirts and blue jeans. They might want to draw sandwiches on their T-shirts with fabric paints.

Figure 4.1

Figure 4.2

Figure 4.3

Figure 4.4

Figure 4.5

Figure 4.6

Figure 4.7

Figure 4.8

The Peanut Butter Kids Chant

Welcome friends
Tall and small
We greet you one
We greet you all.
We're the Peanut Butter Group,
Acting out from nuts to soup!
Stories, songs, and jazzy plays—
Ready now? Take it away!

Story

Note: This story can be told by you, another adult, or an older child. Children play the parts of the goats.

The storyteller asks children if they have ever seen a bread seller walking down the street carrying bread on the top of his head. Explain that in some parts of the world, such as Egypt, men do just that. What happens if the bread is dropped? In Egypt, the bread seller picks up the bread and continues walking down the street. But what if a goat grabs the bread? What can the man do?

The storyteller selects several children in the audience to be the goats in the story. Instruct the goats to come up and take a piece of bread from the seller's head when the story tells them to do this. Also, all the goats will speak this line "Naa! Naa! Naa!" when the bread seller asks for the bread. Now you are ready to tell the story.

Bread for Sale

Once there was a man who sold bread in the market place of Luxor in Egypt. He did not sell the bread from a shop, nor did he transport the bread in a cart. This man was too poor to own a cart. Besides, he was very skilled at carrying the bread of the top of his head.

Egyptian bread is flat, so the man stacked the flat bread on top of his head. Then he walked through the streets as he called, "Bread! Bread for sale. Fifty piasters a piece!"

One morning the man couldn't sell any bread, so he walked out of the dusty marketplace and into the oasis land beside the Nile, where the crops grow green and lush. He saw a date tree nearby and thought to himself, "This is a fine place to take a nap."

The man felt his head. The stack of bread was still there. He sat down under the tree, and he went to sleep. Egyptian days, especially in the summer, are very warm, so the man slept for a long, long time.

Now while the man was asleep, an old billy goat came by, sniffed the bread, and snatched a piece. Another billy goat came by, sniffed the bread, and snatched a piece. Then a nanny goat came by, sniffed the bread, and snatched a piece. Another nanny goat came by, sniffed the bread, and snatched a piece. Finally a little kid goat came by, sniffed the bread, and snatched the last piece.

When the man awoke, he felt rested and ready to walk back to the marketplace. But before he went, he felt the top of his head to be sure the bread was still in place. The bread was gone.

The man looked to the left, and what did he see? No bread!

The man looked to the right, and what did he see? No bread!

The man looked all around, and what did he see? No bread!

Finally, the man looked far beyond the oasis where the sand begins, and what do you think he saw?

Goats! Big goats, middle-sized goats, baby kid goats! And every goat was nibbling a piece of bread.

The man was angry! He looked sternly at the goats. The goats looked sternly at the man. He didn't know what to do. Finally he spoke.

The man shouted, "You goats, you, give me back my bread."

But the goats kept on nibbling and said, "Naa, naa, naaa!"

What was the man going to do?

He shook his fist at the goats and shouted again, "You goats, you, give me back my bread."

But the goats kept on nibbling and said, "Naa, naa, naaa!"

What was the man going to do?

He shook his fist at the goats and shouted again, "You goats, you, give me back my bread."

But the goats shook their hooves at him and said, "Naa, naa, naaa!"

The man shook both hands at the goats and shouted, "You goats, you, give me back my bread."

But the goats shook their hooves again and said, "Naa, naa, naaa!"

Finally the man got so angry that he threw his basket on the ground.

The goats were so scared, they all dropped their bread and ran away.

Then the man picked up his bread, piece by piece. He dusted it off, put it back on his head, and slowly walked back into the market place.

He called, "Bread! Bread for sale! Fifty piasters a piece."

Chorus Line of the Salad Bar

Salad Bar Kids march to front of stage area and stand in front of the audience as they chant the chorus. Each character then steps forward to recite his or her lines. All salad bar characters follow this chant with the "Salad Bar Song."

Chorus Line Characters

Lottie Lettuce, Chuck Celery, Rosie Radish, Carol Carrot, Paul Pepper, Tom Tomato, Olive Olive

Chorus of the Salad Bar

We're the salad
At the bar
Come and try us
As we are!

Come on, put us
On your plate
We're so fresh
We taste just great!

Lettuce: Lettuce, lettuce
Crunch! Crunch! Crunch!

Radish: Rosie Radish
Munch! Munch! Munch!

Celery: Celery Celery
Crunch! Crunch! Crunch!

Carrot: Carrot Carrot
Munch, munch, munch

Pepper: Peppers Peppers
Pick a bunch!

Olive: Olive Olives
Pack a punch!

Tomato: Tomato! Tomato!
For your lunch!

Salad Bar Song

(All veggies then sing the following song to the tune of "My Bonnie Lies over the Ocean")

We welcome you now to our drama
Starring the Salad Bar Troupe
With Cakes and fine cookies to follow
Oh sing with us now in this group.

Chorus: Food for dinner
Bring us our favorite treat, our treat
Food's the best thing
If you are hungry to eat!

The Duet of the Cakes: Angel Food and Devil's Food

Note: Follow instructions under "Procedure" as you prepare to do the cakewalk. Then cakewalk kids to this next song.

Songs to the tune of "My Bonnie Lies over the Ocean"

Angel Food Verse: My Angel Food's out of the oven
There isn't a crumb in the pan
I've mixed up the perfect white frosting
Now wait for a taste if you can.

Chorus: Waiting, Begging
When will we ever receive a bite?
Waiting, begging
For one taste, we'll be
Sweet and nice!

Devil's Food Verse: My Devil's Food messed up the kitchen,
We couldn't resist the sweet smell
The bowl overturned and it splattered
All over the floor when it fell.

Peanut Butter Kids Good-Bye

All kids in the previous stories now come to the front of the stage area and deliver this good-bye chant to the audience. After this, refreshments are served.

This is the end
Of our show,
Thanks for coming,
But, wait—there's more!
We'll serve you snacks
We've all had fun
But now's the time
For YOU to clap!

(The kids bow to the applause).

School Library Setting: Class Cookbook Story Books

Writing cookbooks is an activity the school media specialist can introduce with language arts teachers. Begin this activity by reading food stories and cookbooks to kids and following up with the directions described here.

Materials Needed

1. Suggested food books: *Something's Happening on Calabash Street, Matzah Ball Soup,* and *If You Give a Pig a Pancake*

2. Writing paper and pencils (or word processors) for student writing

3. Recipe cards or index cards

4. Brightly colored construction paper, 11-by-17-inch, enough sheets for each class member to create a cookbook cover

5. Photos of students and their families (optional)

6. Food dishes made at home for potluck at end of project, if desired

Procedure

1. Begin with a favorite food story. Read it to the class and follow up with the suggested activities listed in this section. For example, read aloud *Something's Happening on Calabash Street.* In the story, each family in the neighborhood prepares a different dish to bring to the evening's fiesta. The joyful mood of the story will motivate your students to have a class potluck meal. Tell students to bring a family recipe to class the next day. If the recipe is one a parent or grandparent prepares from memory, all the better. Students then ask the parent to help them write down the steps and the ingredients needed.

2. Ask children to read their recipes aloud. Then share with them the form for writing down a recipe of their own. The recipe pages in *Second Helpings* (Irving and Currie, Teacher Ideas Press, 1994) provide an example of how to list ingredients and then describe the preparation method in a series of steps.

3. Have several children who have brought recipes that are written in this straightforward manner copy their recipes on the blackboard or white board for the whole class to see.

4. Instruct students to write down their own recipes on index cards or on full sheets of paper for the class cookbook.

5. You might want to prepare one simple recipe in class so that everyone understands the concept of writing down a sequence and following those steps. Explain to students that directions and instructions for making things or performing operations use words clearly so that they are easy to follow. This is not as easy to do as it looks!

6. Let children illustrate their recipes or include a family photo on the recipe pages.

7. Photocopy all pages so that all students will have their own copy of the class cookbook.

8. Give each child a large piece of construction paper to decorate for the cover. Provide rubberstamps of food or carve potatoes to make your own stamps, dipping them into paint to make potato-print covers.

9. Plan a day for a class potluck with family food dishes provided from home. Encourage recipes from different ethnic groups. A Chinese family might bring homemade egg rolls or dumplings. A Mexican family might bring homemade tamales. An African American family might bring peanut butter soup or a type of soul food. Children of a Western European background that they may not identify with can bring a family favorite or any food they enjoy. My Grandma O'Neal, for example, was famous for her country custard pie. My children might bring a pie they made with my help, or a commercial custard pie from the grocery dairy case if Mom was too busy to bake with them.

Cook-Off Stories

The next writing activity focuses on story writing using a cooking competition model. Discuss the term "cook-off" with students as you give examples of companies that have food contests. The finalists often come to a place for the last competition in which they have a cook-off and make their own dishes.

The following activity is based on reading the book *Matzah Ball Soup* by Joan Rothenberg.

Procedure

1. Read the book *Matzah Ball Soup* by Joan Rothenberg. On the board, write the differences in the recipes discussed in the book. (Example: one aunt uses onion in her recipe, another aunt uses bread crumbs in hers.)

2. Ahead of time, find several versions of the same food. Good examples are barbeque sauce, green chili, spaghetti sauce.

3. Select one food to plan a class story. Write a rough outline of the story on the board so that students will understand steps in creating a story by a using a model or example. I have provided a model in this section.

The Fortellini Family Food Feud

Recipe: Spaghetti Sauce

Basic ingredient: Tomatoes

Variations of the Four Fortellini Brothers

Basil and onion	Frank
Cheese, oregano	Joey
Green peppers	Mike
Garlic	Giovanni

Story Line: Four brothers all bring spaghetti sauce to the family reunion. Each is proud of his recipe. A family feud begins when Frank's son Frankie tastes his father's sauce and exclaims, "My father's sauce is the best." Each child tastes a different sauce and declares it is the best. The whole family gets into an argument. How will this predicament end?

Class Discussion:

1. Talk through the process described here. Ask students to suggest possible endings and write these on the board. For example:

   • The family members start slinging spaghetti at each other and everyone leaves angry.

   • They each taste all the sauces and dump them together to make one big sauce.

   • The argument gets so loud that the neighbors call the police. The police choose the best sauce.

   • Grandma Fortellini begs for silence and comes up with the best solution. All four sauces are so good that everyone should enjoy them. Next year, Giovanni will bring his sauce; the following year, Mike will bring his sauce; the third year, Joey will bring his sauce; and the fourth year, Frank will bring his.

2. Students choose among the four endings and write their own stories.

"If You Give . . ." Food Stories

Laura Numeroff's popular series beginning with *If You Give a Mouse a Cookie* has inspired teachers to use this model of logical outcomes for creative writing. If you have not done this, explore this model with your students using the following example.

If You Give a Cow a Pizza

Situation: The cow gets a pizza.

Outcome: The cow eats the pizza slowly.

Then: A faster animal, such as a cat, steals the rest of the pizza and its box.

Then: The cat drags the pizza and box to an alley where . . .

Outcome: The trash man picks up the empty box, looks at it, and drives to the Pizza shop to order his own pizza. Unfortunately, he . . .

Then: dumps his trash outside the pizza shop.

Then: All the customers in the pizza shop rummage through the trash.

Then: The city is filled with things the citizens tried to throw away.

Outcomes: Mrs. Martin sees Matt's missing tennis shoe on the stack so Matt can play ball again.
Molly McGee finds her lost kitten.
Farmer McIntosh finds a coupon for a free pizza and

Ending: Farmer McIntosh takes his coupon for a free pizza to the pizza shop the next day. He eats all of the pizza except for one piece, which he feeds to his old cow Bessie. And the cow eats the pizza.

There are no "rules" for setting up your own sequence, except that this is a "circle story"—the end should bring the reader back to the beginning. In this case, I needed to find a way for the cow to get another piece of pizza at the end of the story.

Idea Springboards: Activities to Develop

Food Poem Mural

The book *Food Fight* features food poems written by noted children's poets, contributed to aid Share Our Strength, an organization devoted to combating world hunger. Read samples from this delightful book as inspiration for children to write their own food poems. Note that many of the poems rhyme, others are in special verse forms such as haiku and use free verse.

Stretch a long piece of art paper or brown wrapping paper to the wall, and then glue or tape individual poems to make your own food mural.

Ask student artists to illustrate the poems.

Food Art

Book illustrations inspire children's food art. Here are a few ideas for you to begin your own class projects.

1. Give each student a paper plate, bright colors of construction paper, glue, and scissors. Encourage them to cut out food shapes to glue on the plates. Illustrations from Lois Ehlert's books with simple graphic shapes are good models.

2. Give students food and wood kabob skewers to make stick puppets out of food. Examples: orange-head creatures with cabbage leaf ears and red-pepper mouths; apple-head monsters with teeth made from corn kernels.

3. Give students brightly colored clay to make food inspired by the book *Still-Life Stew*.

5
Storytelling Sampler

Books and Activities about Storytelling

Some of the chapters in this book focus on themes such as art, and others, such as this one, center on skills. Excellent storytelling books and tapes have been created especially in the past decade. Collections of stories from famous storytellers and storytelling associations fill library shelves. Why should I add my voice?

Like many of you, I have been a professional storyteller for a long time—more than twenty-five years. Actually, I have been a storyteller all of my life. I think this is true for most of you. This may surprise many, but I have reminded teachers, students, and librarians in workshops and classrooms that I believe we tell stories every day of our lives. Perhaps we are not conscious of this, but every time we relate an episode or incident that has happened to us, we are storytellers.

Every storyteller has a different voice or approach worth sharing with other storytellers. With this base, I'd like to share ways I have found to incorporate storytelling into your library programs and classroom activities. I enjoy mentoring new storytellers and guiding them through the early stages in which they gain confidence. I will share experiences I've had as a teacher who used storytelling with high school students who were turned off by school because they could barely read. Author and storyteller Craig Rooney writes that he became a storyteller to survive a teaching job working with troubled teens.

Storytelling, even more than reading stories, has the power to change lives. A celebrated librarian and storyteller from Iowa tells her audiences, "Stories [and storytelling] have saved my life." Even if you don't see yourself as a "storytelling lifesaver," you can reach young people in a deeper way if you look into children's eyes as you begin to tell a story. This may sound scary, but I challenge you to take the plunge—it's worth it!

Young children are natural storytellers. They shape events in their lives around people (characters) and actions. Some flesh out the basic narrative with dialogue, descriptive details, and settings. These inchoate stories may ramble, digress, or stumble, but you can guide this story process.

Build on children's oral accounts, ask them questions to clarify and expand. Talk through story episodes. Read and tell them basic folktales that build on repeated sequences. Help them see clearly defined patterns in "The Three Little Pigs," "The Three Bears," and "The Three Billy Goats Gruff." Second and third graders can learn to tell these tales to kindergarteners with fluency and flourish. Fourth- and fifth-grade students are ready to form storytelling clubs. The older students gain self-confidence and develop important language skills. Younger students learn stories quickly from "older" models, and, more important, they respect stories in a powerful way.

Seize the moment to pause during a reading lesson to tell students a story. Suppose you are teaching a unit about communities. Take time to tell a simple version of the folktale "Stone Soup" to demonstrate how people can work together to share their resources so that all will survive. A math problem about speed can be enhanced with a retelling of Aesop's "The Tortoise and the Hare." Just think! Storytelling can guide your entire teaching career.

School media specialists can teach library skills by telling a short story about the Loch Ness monster as they show the range of books in the Dewey classification marked 000. Direct kids who enjoy trivial facts by telling an episode from *So You Want to Be President* as you head toward the 973.09 area about American History.

Public library youth librarians are in the habit of telling stories in preschool story hours. Don't forget you can introduce a school-age program in which a magician will perform by telling "Rumpelstiltskin" as straw is turned into gold. Ask middle school students to join you in telling ghost stories for older elementary students. Even self-conscious young teens are willing to tell stories in a semidark room if they are asked to tell "scary stories." Use stories in family story settings. By all means, offer programs on crafts and puppet making, but don't forget to tuck in a story along the way. Tell "How Spider Obtained the Sky God's Stories," as children do a weaving project or making the dream catchers described in the springboards section of this chapter.

If you're ready to start telling stories, perhaps this little acronym will help you begin:

Select the story by reading many folktales and collections of simple stories

Tell the story you've read out loud to yourself

Over and over again.

Remember the main action sequences

(Make it . . .) **Y**ours

In selecting the story, read widely, and listen to storytellers on tape. Find a story that you really like, so you will naturally infuse your telling with enthusiasm. I recommend beginning with folktales that have clear-cut sequences and beginning-middle-end structures. I like stories with a sense of the dramatic and humorous tales. Maybe sinister tales are appealing to you. Listening to tapes will guide you in using various vocal inflections, pauses, and overall timing.

As you begin to tell the story to yourself, visualize the setting and allow yourself to step into the characters of the story. You may wish to go back and read the story several times before you are comfortable telling it even to yourself. Visual learners may draw the sequences in a rough cartoon strip. Verbal learners may write down the sequences or tell the sequences before they tell much as a diver thinks through the physical act of diving before he jumps.

Do this telling over and over again until the pattern is comfortable, and you can use your own words to retell the story. If there are repeated refrains, you will want to memorize these. Practice the beginning and ending so they are well polished, but tell the story until you feel at ease improvising the story itself. Storytelling, unless you've chosen an authored tale such as one of Carl Sandburg's *Rootabaga Stories*, is not dramatic recitation or the acting out of memorized lines. Allow yourself to show through.

Now you are making the story "yours." Add words and gestures, if you like, to help your audience see the setting. If you're ready, give the characters facial expressions and body movements. Some of us speak with hand gestures and actions so naturally that to stay still with hands behind our backs would cramp our telling. If you are less animated, try a little more action, but do what seems comfortable.

I caution storytellers to avoid slang expressions unless they are compatible with the style of the story. You don't have to simplify your telling with "controlled vocabularies" found in beginning readers because young children are your audience. Give them the benefit of learning new words and stretching their minds. Perhaps two of the most important things to keep in mind are speaking slowly and loudly enough for people to grasp the story. Take time to pause, use a moment of silence, especially as you are leading to an important phrase or climax of the story. Women, beware! High-pitched voices grate the nerves. My mother, an effective storyteller and amateur actress, chided me at an early age to modulate my voice.

The bibliography that follows this section notes a few collections of stories and single stories for storytellers. The resource bibliography at the end of the book lists professional books about the art of storytelling.

Books of Stories for Storytellers

Bunting, Eve. *The Memory String*. Illus. Ted Rand. Clarion, 2000.

Laura is struggling to come to terms with her mother's death. She clings to memories represented by buttons on a string. Although this story is not about storytelling per se, it becomes a metaphor for remembering stories with a kind of storytelling memory device.

Caduto, Michael, and Joseph Bruchac. *Keepers of the Night*. Fulcrum, 1994.

These two writers have written several books in the "Keepers" series. This one is a collection of Native American stories and nocturnal activities for children. Several stories, such as "The Creation of the Moon," are mentioned in this chapter. Science activities accompany the native legends. These books are wonderful additions to science and storytelling programs.

Cohlene, Terri. *Quillworker, a Cheyenne Legend*. Illus. Charles Reasoner. Rourke/Watermill Press, 1990.

One of the Native American Legends series, this legend explains the origins of stars. Facts about the Cheyenne people accompany the text.

Coyote & Bobcat. Illus. Kathy Kifer and Dahna Solar. Garlic Press, 1996.

Part of the Sign Language Literature Series, this Navajo story is adapted in simple language with illustrated sign language signs to enrich the basic tale.

Dayrell, Elphinstone Dayrell. *Why the Sun and the Moon Live in the Sky*. Houghton Mifflin, 1968.

This adaptation of an old African folktale about the origins of the world tells how Sun and Moon were forced to live in the sky because Water and all its people came to call, causing them to move to the roof of their house and then up into the sky. This short tale works for beginning storytellers and for those who wish to adapt it as interactive storytelling with many children taking parts.

Duncan, Lois. *The Magic of Spider Woman*. Illus. Shonto Begay. Scholastic, 1995.

This Navajo legend of the Spider Woman, who learns to keep her life in balance through the boundaries of spinning wisely is a metaphor for the skill of spinning stories. This one is recommended for more advanced storytellers or as an inspiration to all storytellers.

Galdone, Joanna. *The Tailypo, a Ghost Story*. Illus. Paul Galdone. Clarion Books, 1977.

This Appalachian story about an old man who chops off the tail of a scary creature invading his house only to suffer consequences is a much-beloved tale for beginning and experienced storytellers. Look for many retellings of folktales by Paul Galdone in your library.

Goble, Paul. *Her Seven Brothers*. Bradbury Press, 1988.

Another version of the Cheyenne legend (see Cohlene, *Quillworker*) explains how the Big Dipper is created. An Indian girl searches for her seven brothers, and on finding them gives them beaded shirts. Together the girl and her brothers escape from a buffalo stampede and ascend into the sky, where they become stars.

Haley, Gail. *A Story, a Story*. Atheneum, 1970.

This popular Caldecott Medal book tells the classic West African story in which Anansi spins a web to the sky to plea for the Sky God's golden box of stories. Anansi agrees to perform three feats in order to receive the box, which he then takes back to earth to share with all people.

Hamilton, Virginia. *The Girl Who Spun Gold*. Illus. Leo and Diane Dillon. Blue Sky Press/ Scholastic, 2000.

Hamilton's West Indian variation of the English tale "Tom Tit Tot" or the German "Rumpelstiltskin" is a tale of magic featuring spinning and trickery. It can also be a metaphor for the spinning of story. Use this version or a simpler one as a model for students to begin a storytelling unit.

Holt, David, and Bill Mooney. *Spiders in the Hairdo: Modern Urban Legends*. August House, 1999.

Humorous and grotesque stories inspired by urban legends are retold by two of America's popular storytellers. They are short and simple enough for beginners to tell, and the subject matter delights older kids who like offbeat stories. The publisher is known for its many storytelling collections.

MacDonald, Margaret Read. *Shake-It-Up Tales!: Stories to Sing, Dance, Drum, and Act Out*. August House, 2000.

Prolific author and beloved storyteller MacDonald creates this collection of singing and dancing tales from all over the world. Look for her other story collections.

Martin, Jr., Bill, and John Archambault. *Knots on a Counting Rope*. Illus. Ted Rand. Holt, 1987.

A Native American boy urges his blind grandfather to tell again the story of the boy's birth as the old man makes another knot in his storytelling rope.

McDermott, Gerald. *Coyote*. Harcourt Brace, 1994.

In this adaptation of the Navajo legend, Coyote wishes to fly like the crows. He tricks them into giving him feathers and then tries to dance like them, but he boasts so much that the crows take away his feathers. Coyote falls to the earth, turns brown like the dust, but never gives up his tricky ways.

Musgrove, Margaret. *The Spider Weaver: A Legend of Kente Cloth*. Illus. Julia Cairns. Blue Sky/Scholastic, 2001.

This story from Ghana tells the story of the creation of Kente cloth. This connects African legends about spiders that share the task of weaving and about people telling stories.

Oughton, Jerrie. *How the Stars Fell into the Sky: A Navajo Legend*. Illus. Lisa Desimini. Houghton Mifflin, 1992.

In this Navajo legend, a young woman uses the night sky to write her laws of the land. Coyote agrees to help, but he creates chaos when he impatiently throws her stars into the sky against her careful plans. This is a good introduction to telling star stories with children.

Taback, Simms. *Joseph Had a Little Overcoat*. Viking, 1999.

This Caldecott Medal winner uses folk art and die cuts to tell the tale of a tailor who refashions his coat into other garments as each part wears out. The story is a model for storytellers who retell a story in their own way. Read the book, then encourage children to retell the tale in their own words. This is a good book for beginning tellers.

Wilder, Laura Ingalls. *On the Banks of Plum Creek*. Harper, 1941, 1953.

The draw-and-tell story described in the chapter "A Day of Games" is one delightful episode from the autobiographical novel about the Ingalls family and their lives in Walnut Creek, Minnesota.

Xiong, Blia. *Nine-in-One Grr! Grr!* Children's Book Press, 1989.

With the assistance of storyteller Cathy Spagnoli, this Hmong writer tells a delightful trickster tale about a bird who tricks Tiger so that not too many tigers will inhabit the earth.

Yolen, Jane, ed. *Favorite Folktales from around the World*. Pantheon/Random House, 1986.

Yolen, a prolific writer and storyteller in her own right, has selected dozens of folktales and arranged them by themes into thirteen chapters. Storytellers will want to add this exhaustive resource to their story collections.

Zelinsky, Paul. *Rumpelstiltskin*. Dutton, 1986.

This beautiful retelling of the classic Grimm tale about spinning straw into gold simply glow with Zelinsky's brilliant illustrations. Use this story and other versions of this folktale for programs on spinning and storytelling.

Note: Libraries Unlimited has published many storytelling collections worth discovering. In particular, look for the numerous titles in its World Folklore Series.

Storytelling Programs

Storytelling Festival

Stage a festival during the summer on the library lawn or in a park. You will draw a crowd with a rented tent, or you can simply decorate the lawn. The festival will last about an hour to an hour and a half. Note that the following procedure offers alternatives to stage the festival inside if you wish.

The festival consists of several parts. In the main tent, "performance storytellers" who are experienced will tell stories to the larger audience. Story-sharing circles are set up at a distance from the tent for beginning storytellers or for those who wish to engage in impromptu storytelling. Add a coat rack or hat tree to one circle for a puppet circle or a "Puppet-tree." A refreshment table is set up for everyone's enjoyment.

Materials Needed

1. A large open tent or tarp, rented or borrowed (Grocers, garden centers, and many churches own their own tents if you can't rent one from a rental store.)

2. Drapes, or about five yards of material to drape across a wall for indoor events

3. A spinning wheel borrowed from a local spinner or yarn shop (optional, but nice)

4. Assortments of puppets to help tell stories (Many libraries have puppets to check out. If you don't have access to a collection, ask children to bring their own puppets to the festival.)

5. A coat rack or hat tree, borrowed (If not available, a large basket of puppets will work.)

6. Posterboard, several sticks, tape, markers for yard signs

7. Drum, any kind you can borrow (even a toy drum will work)

8. Dozens of blankets, borrowed from anyone, or ask participants to bring their own

9. A small box and slips of paper on which to write story starters

10. Pitchers of water and paper cups and other light refreshments if desired

Procedure

The Main Tent

1. If you have a spinning wheel, place it just outside the tent. A sign tells people that the sign of a spinning wheel outside the tent or a house traditionally announced the appearance of a storyteller in past times. If you don't have a spinning wheel, draw a picture of one on your sign. Puppeteers and mimes could mingle with people coming to your festival.

2. When the performing storytellers are ready, one teller beats the drum and calls out, "Lo, the storytellers come! Beat the drums/Gentle folk gather round/Come! Come!"

3. Audience proceeds to tent; and they are welcomed and ushered inside by tellers and mimes.

4. If the event is outside, provide blankets to spread on the ground and a few lawn chairs for people who need them. Arrange stools and canvas chairs in front for the tellers. The main teller welcomes the audience and announces each teller.

5. You can determine the length of your program, but I recommend limiting this event to one hour or less. For variety, I recommend having two to four people tell stories to accommodate the varying attention spans of audience members.

Story Circles

1. Designate three story circles with posterboard signs stuck into the ground. Add blankets for the comfort of each group.

2. Designate a leader for each group. Circle One is for beginning tellers to share stories they know or are learning at the time. The leader begins with a tale then asks for volunteers to tell their tales.

3. Circle Two is devoted to impromptu stories using a Story Sampler Box. Write story starters on slips of paper or index cards and put in a box for participants to select from. This sampler box is prepared ahead of time. For extra fun, use a candy sampler box and add your own "Story Sampler" label to the top of the box. The following samples can inspire your own story samples.

Sample I: A Finger in Every Pie

Need: Six people

Starter: Peter (or Polly) Pumpkin Eater enters a pie-baking contest. Determined to win, he sabotages everyone's pie by poking his finger in the corner of all the pies to "spoil them." Then he wipes his finger on his shirt. Play the part of Peter, draft four bakers and one judge to act out this story. Make up your own dialogue as the bakers enter the contest and Peter does his dirty deed. What does the Judge do? Does he name Peter the winner? Do the other bakers convince the judge that Peter is up to dirty tricks? What happens?

Sample II: All but One

Need: Six noodleheads, one Super Noodle

Starter: Six noodleheads go swimming. When they get out of the water, the first noodlehead says he hopes no one drowns. The second noodlehead suggests they count noses. The third noodlehead counts everyone, but forgets to count himself. All cry. The fourth noodlehead repeats the action. All cry. The fifth noodlehead counts everyone again, as the third and fourth have. All cry. The sixth noodlehead runs off to bring in Super Noodle. Super Noodle counts all six. Everyone cheers that the lost one is found. Act this out with your own dialogue.

Create about ten more story starters. Use story collections or simple folktales, such as "The Three Sillies" for inspiration. This story may be found in the Yolen collection listed in the bibliography.

4. Circle Three is set up like the other story circles, but in this area your sign will read "Puppet Corner." The leader passes out puppets to play roles of the various characters in the story. The leader or several people may tell the tales. Older children may wish to do the telling of familiar stories such as "The Bremen Town Musicians," "The Enormous Turnip," or "The Little Red Hen." Plan the stories around puppets you have or can borrow from libraries, schools, and teachers and librarians.

5. The Main Storyteller of the Day moves from circle to circle for about thirty minutes during the story circle time.

Ending the Storytelling Festival

1. At the end of the story circle time, the main storyteller bangs the drum, and announces: "Lo the stories have come and gone/remember them all, then pass them on!"

2. After the event that will last about one to one and a half hours, as people leave, provide cups of water and a light snack such as fruit and crackers if you wish.

Storytelling Festival: Indoor Alternative

Materials

Same as in outdoor version

Procedure

1. Create a storyteller's corner with a curtain hung across one corner of the room or simply hang fabric across a wall, draping it as you like.

2. Set up story circles by placing blankets and signs around the room in a similar fashion to the descriptions for the outside version of this activity.

3. If you have more than one large room, you may wish to set up the story circles in other rooms.

4. Let your main storyteller or the leader begin and end the event in the same way suggested for the outside activity.

Storytelling in School Classrooms

Schools frequently invite guest storytellers to perform for young audiences. Youth librarians in public libraries often tell stories, but many do not have time to leave their own work environment to perform in schools. Ask librarians if they know any professional storytellers who could come to your school. These tellers need to be paid, but local people can sometimes offer special prices or help you find funds to offset the cost.

This full-scale program will encourage you to incorporate stories in the school curriculum. Sometimes the school media specialist plans this activity. If a teacher brings her language arts class, for example, to the library, the media person might show the children the folktale collection shelved under the Dewey number 398.2. She would then gather the class around her to tell a traditional tale such as "Talk," or "The Three Sillies." (Note that both of these stories can be found in the collection by Jane Yolen listed in the bibliography to this chapter.)

Schools open to using stories throughout the curriculum will enlist the help of the school media specialist or a teacher familiar with storytelling to use stories in these various settings.

Stories in the Arts

In ancient times, storytelling and drama were combined with dance, music, and the artistry of masks in a seamless celebration. Hearken back to these days with classroom or schoolwide productions combining these arts. The following ideas can help art, music, language arts, and physical education teachers work with students.

An African Story Play Combining Storytelling, Creative Dramatics, Art, and Music

Materials Needed

1. Posterboard in basic colors, construction paper, plain paper plates

2. Thin elastic cording for masks, about two to three feet per mask

3. Craft sticks for masks, about two dozen

4. Three overhead transparencies and three permanent markers in brown, blue, and green

5. An overhead projector

6. Tape of African music or music students playing thumb pianos and drums to create sound effects at important parts of story

Procedure

1. Ask your art teacher to guide children in making their own posterboard or paper-plate African masks. The illustrations in *Why the Sun and the Moon Live in the Sky* by Blair Lent can help children develop their own ideas. If you want to encourage children stretch their visual imagination, simply cut out yellow posterboard circles (eight to ten inches in diameter), and a white posterboard diamond shape (ten to twelve inches in length). Blue and green posterboard fish shapes about eight to ten inches long can be precut.

2. Allow children thirty minutes to one hour to make their masks. Punch holes in the sides of the masks and stretch elastic cording through the holes. Tie knots to secure the cord in the holes.

3. Draw a small grass hut on one transparency, and a larger hut on another transparency, and a very big hut on the third transparency.

4. Consult the music teacher to provide music tapes of African music, borrow percussion instruments, and invite music classes to practice rhythmical songs. This music can introduce the storytelling. You might simply borrow the instruments and guide children in creating their own sounds to add musical effects to the storytelling.

5. Tell this African legend or guide a student storyteller in telling the story to a group of children. After the story is told, ask children to put on their masks, and instruct them to move as the story is being told.

6. Place the first transparency on an overhead projector and dim the lights.

7. The story begins. I suggest the Sun and Water characters sit on stools at the beginning of the story. Water leaves the scene, and then Sun walks over to Moon, who is standing slightly to the left.

8. Project the second transparency behind them. When Sun and Moon start building the new house, remove the transparencies and allow the characters to mime the act of building a house. Then place the third transparency on the projector. Have Sun beckon Water to return to the stage area.

9. Water then beckons all of his people to come visit Sun and Moon in their new house. The musicians play "water music" or a gentle rhythms on their instruments. The water people carry their fish masks (cardboard shapes mounted on craft sticks) and dance as in a procession around the room and up to the stage area.

10. As the water people take over the stage, instruct Sun and Moon to stand on the stools. As the music and movement reach a crescendo, Sun and Moon raise their arms above their heads and wave them as if they are flying into the sky.

11. At the end of the story, all story participants hum "Ah-ummmmm." The storyteller ends by telling the audience, "My story is done. Ah—um. Stories begin and stories end. Tell this one over. Ah—um, ah—um!"

Note: Because many tribes in Africa have used masks and music as part of the story experience, you can choose other folktales to adapt in this manner. Gail Haley's West African story titled *A Story, a Story* or any Anansi story are good choices for this activity.

Stories in History Settings: Westward Expansion

Elementary school children study the westward expansion, the Civil War, pioneer days, and building communities at various grade levels and in the context of a variety of topics. This program builds on the theme of expansion and can be adapted as you like.

Materials Needed

1. A roll of brown wrapping paper

2. Brown and black markers

3. Pioneer and Native American objects to display (Examples might include Navajo rugs and baskets, a coyote statue or drawing, pioneer hats, tin plates, slates or small chalkboards and chalk.)

4. Copies of Laura Ingalls Wilder's *On the Banks of Plum Creek,* McDermott's *Coyote* and *Coyote and Bobcat;* display of other books about the historical period from about 1849 to 1870, including fiction and picture books set during this time period

5. Maps of the United States from this period of history, or a U.S. map from a more recent period

6. Tapes of American folk songs or a musician who knows folk songs from this period (Specific songs you might use include "Old Dan Tucker," "She'll Be Comin' Round the Mountain," and "Skip to My Lou"; also use tapes of Native American flute music.)

Procedure

1. Make time lines from the time period about 1849 to 1870. Stretch brown wrapping paper around the library or classroom. Use markers to designate important events that you will be studying or introducing to children. Label your time line "History and Stories during the Days of American Expansion." Suggestions for your time line might include these events:

    • **1849** Gold discovered in California, the Gold Rush begins

    • **1851** First American military post built in Navajo territory, present-day Arizona

    • **1860** Abraham Lincoln is elected president of the United States

    • **1861** The Civil War begins

    • **1862** The Homestead Act is passed, encouraging people to settle land on the frontier

- **1863–64** Kit Carson battles Navajos in Arizona

- **1865** The Civil War ends

- **1867** Laura Ingalls is born

- **1868** The Navajo Treaty with United States brings peace

- **1870s** During a period of increasing western expansion, the Ingalls family begins their pioneer journeys. Pioneer and tall tales are shared among people traveling west. Native peoples tell their stories as well.

2. Intersperse the history lesson or discussion of events shown in the time line with stories from both White and Navajo traditions.

3. Begin with a folk song such as "Buffalo Gals" or "Home on the Range." You might also choose to tell a Navajo trickster tale about Coyote. Two appropriate stories appear in the bibliography of this chapter. McDermott's *Coyote* can be read and then told with children enacting the parts of the crows and coyote. *Coyote and Bobcat* adds another interesting way of communicating by adapting Native American sign language to help children discover a form of telling stories beyond oral language.

4. Give children some background about author Laura Ingalls Wilder, whom they probably know already through the television series and her "Little House" books. Retell the "draw-and-tell" story Ma tells the girls in the chapter "A Day of Games" from *On the Banks of Plum Creek*. This draw-and-tell story was a diversion from the hard work of pioneer days.

5. Read or tell a tall tale from this time period, such as a story about Pecos Bill.

6. Have students tell their own original tall tales for a further extension of this lesson.

Stories in a Science Setting: Sun, Moon, and Starry Nights

Stories from the Amazon enhance science lessons about tropical rainforests. Animal stories become natural adjuncts to science and nature lessons. This program unit combines stories about the sun, moon, and stars with some basic science activities.

Materials Needed

1. Black construction paper, several boxes of silver adhesive stars, a box of white chalk

2. A flashlight, a large green Styrofoam ball for the earth, a smaller Styrofoam ball painted silver

3. A strand of small, white Christmas lights

4. Copies of Oughton's *How the Stars Fell into the Sky*, Cohlene's *Quillworker* or Goble's *Her Seven Brothers*, and Bruchac's *Keepers of the Night*, as well as other books about sun, moon, and stars from your library collection (both fiction and nonfiction)

Procedure

Part I

1. Darken the classroom or simply dim the lights to create a night setting. Plug in the Christmas lights and ask two children to stretch them at waist height against a wall. Children hold the lights during the telling of the first story.

2. Begin with one of the star stories listed in the bibliography, such as *How the Stars Fell into the Sky*. The story can be read or told.

3. Turn on the lights again to begin a science lesson on stars and constellations.

4. Have children make Big Dipper or Ursa Major constellation pictures. Give each student a piece of black construction paper. Make your own sample with gummed stars and trace the outline of the dipper with white chalk. Children make their own star dippers. If you wish, they may make other constellations and look for stars in this pattern in the night sky.

5. Invite another storyteller or reader to share one of the two versions of a Cherokee star legend found in the bibliography. Goble's *Her Seven Brothers* is essentially the same story found in Cohlene's *Quillworker.*

6. Have children physically move into constellation patterns around the classroom to understand star formations kinesthetically.

7. You may end the lesson for the day here or proceed into the next section on Sun and Moon.

Part II

1. Begin with the science lesson about sun and moon by dimming the lights. Have Child stand in the middle of the room holding a flashlight. This child becomes the sun. Discuss how the sun rotates around the moon by handing another child the large, white ball and instruct her to walk around the sun in her orbit. After one trip around the sun, the "earth" begins to rotate the ball on its axis. Discuss day and night as students literally see how this happens through the demonstration.

2. Now give the smaller ball to a third child. Instruct the child to move in an orbit around the earth as it moves more slowly around the sun. When the moon passes between the earth and sun, tell the moon to stop momentarily. Tell children this is the arrangement during a solar eclipse.

3. Have the "moon" continue rotating around the earth. When the moon is lined up with the earth and sun, ask the child role-playing the moon to pause, then explain to the class that this is the pattern of the heavenly bodies during a lunar eclipse.

4. Tell a sun and moon tale such as "The Creation of the Moon" found in *Keepers of the Night.*

5. As a follow-up activity, suggest that children grow a common houseplant, such as philoden-dron, in full sunlight and another in semidarkness. This might be a classroom project. At the end of a month, note differences in the plants' growth and discuss the effects of sun on growing things. Retell one of the stories in this lesson.

Idea Springboards: Activities to Develop

Weaving a Yarn, Spinning a Tale

Many English expressions combine storytelling and cloth-making terms. Build on this idea to plan stories and activities about spinning and weaving. Invite a weaver and a spinner to your library or school to demonstrate their skills. Next, tell one of the Spider Woman stories found in the bibliography.

As a follow-up activity make dreamcatchers, using willow branches or grapevines soaked in water overnight, strong string or yarn, beads, and feathers. The illustrations (Figs. 5.1–5.3) will show you a sample dreamcatcher.

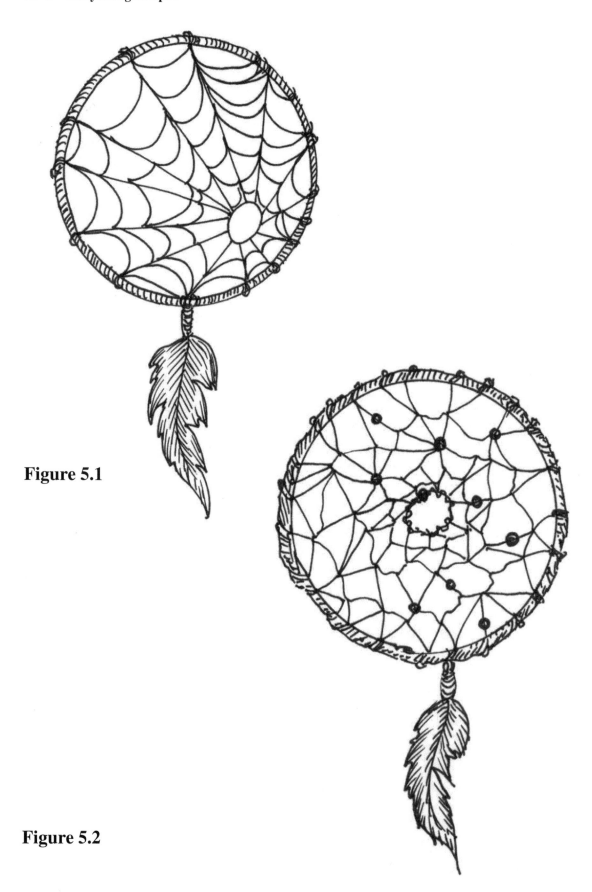

Figure 5.1

Figure 5.2

Figure 5.3

Golden Box of Stories

Gail Haley's *A Story, a Story* describes a golden box of stories that belonged to the Sky God, who kept them under his throne. The small man Anansi weaves a web to the sky and bargains with the Sky God to perform three or four tasks to obtain the story box. Once the tasks are completed, Anansi claims these and brings the stories back to earth to share with all the people.

To create your own golden story box, paint a cigar box or small shoebox gold. Glue felt or velvet inside box. Add small objects that relate to stories you are prepared to tell. A pack of turnip seeds, for example, reminds children of "The Enormous Turnip" found in Sheila Dailey's *Putting the World in a Nutshell* (see Resource Bibliography at end of book). A piece of *kente* cloth or fabric printed to resemble *kente* relates to *The Spider Weaver* by Musgrove. A button captures the spirit of *Joseph Had a Little Overcoat*.

Make your own box to use with students or have students make their own story boxes. Children can add a button for each book they read or draw a picture relating to a story they have read or can tell back to you.

Picture That: Telling Stories from Family Photographs

Teachers use the topic of families in social studies units and assign oral history projects. Youth librarians plan family storytelling events. This activity is perfect for either setting.

Ask each child or family to bring a family photograph that has a story behind it. Think of holiday pictures, vacation pictures, or special events. Doesn't everyone have at least one picture of Dad carving a Thanksgiving turkey or Mom creating a fancy jack-o'-lantern for Halloween?

Help children focus on an interesting beginning to the story they will tell. Guide them in providing a few details. For example: "Last Thanksgiving my dad found the fattest turkey in the grocery store. It was so big, none of us could carry it out of the store alone. Both Mom and Dad had to carry the turkey together." Then talk through several episodes in the story. For example: Getting the turkey home, finding a pot or pan big enough in which to put the turkey, trying to decide when to begin baking the turkey so dinner will be on time, and finally, getting the turkey out of the oven without dropping it.

Explain to children that they are leading up to the climax or high point of the story. Help children think of a dramatic way to tell this part of the story. Encourage them to expand on the truth to create a sense of drama. "Dad and Mom together huffed and puffed, and they finally pulled the turkey out of the oven. They heaved it on top of the stove. Dad thought the turkey looked done. It was brown outside. He took a long carving knife out of the kitchen drawer and started sawing off a hunk at the end. Saw. Saw. Saw. The knife sawing was not going very well. Mom poked the turkey. Blood came out."

Finally, instruct children to create a strong ending for the story so that it seems complete. Remember, you are allowed to vary a bit from the truth. "Mom was so mad because the whole family was starving. The rest of the meal was on the table. So she picked up the turkey, stuffed it into the microwave, and turned the power on high. The turkey exploded! Well, I thought it was going to explode, but it didn't. It cooked that turkey right down to the bone. When Dad took it out and put it on the platter, he sawed again. His knife went right through the meat, and we all had turkey for Thanksgiving. You know, it wasn't too bad, either."

Because children tend to ramble when they tell about personal experiences, this activity will be a great aid in learning to tell a story.

In libraries, divide the audience into small groups, then invite the storytelling to begin. The leader of each group might share a story using the steps described here. Volunteers can tell their own stories. After their telling, the leader suggests ways to reshape the story. In public settings, less interference may be appropriate. In school settings, the teacher or media specialist can work more directly with children. In either setting, encourage participants to gather photographs and tell others about the stories in their own lives.

6
The Poetry Place

Books and Activities about Poetry

If you were a lucky child, someone read, chanted, or even whispered little verses in your ear. Perhaps you can still remember them. Listen to the lines in your mind that sing out:

This is the house that Jack built

This is the malt that lay in the house that Jack built.

This is the rat that ate the malt that lay in the house that Jack built.

Wee Willie Winkie

Runs through the town

Upstairs, downstairs

In his nightgown . . .

Out came the doctor

Out came the nurse

Out came the lady

With the alligator purse

It's likely that you grew up with some of these rhythms and rhymes bouncing in your head. The cadence of Mother Goose is a building block that prepares children to hear more advanced poetry penned by the great English poets. The clapping out of jump-rope rhymes joins one generation to the next in the basic pattern of our American folklore. People, all around the world, respond to rhythm and cadence in different ways. Children especially are tuned into rhythms of nature. Infants know the lub-dub beat of the heart from their time inside the mother's womb. Toddlers listen to the sound of a cricket, a cow, or a crowing rooster. They repeat these sounds over and over again.

Children are also sound-making machines, open to the ding-dongs, pitter-patters, and the hush-hushes they hear. They babble and play with the words we speak to them. Children are poets at heart. We need only nurture this natural response to a world with which children are intimate.

In times past, adults recited poetry they had memorized. My paternal grandfather had a wonderful memory for poems he had learned as a child. Some of my earliest memories go back to the hours I sat on Grandpa's knee, he in his rocking chair, reciting Longfellow, Wordsworth, or a poem of his own making. My grandparents later reminded me that I could recite all of " 'Twas the Night Before Christmas" when I was just two years old. My father returned from the army during World War II eager to teach me how to make up rhymes. My first attempts were unsuccessful, but his persistence paid off. I soon loved words, rhythm, and rhyme and enjoyed playing with them. I still do. I remember verses from Shakespeare, the Brownings, Longfellow, and even "long losts" such as William Cullen Bryant that I learned as an older child.

I know that today's educators consider it passé to require students to memorize and recite poetry, and I have seen adults struggle to commit poetry to memory. I can understand the frustration and resentment many people feel when strapped into the straightjacket of memorization. And I know plenty of adults who declare they hate poetry because of their past experiences with it. Forced to read fussy verse or didactic lines, the poetry to which they were exposed had no impact on their lives. They had to "pick it apart" for meaning.

Well-meaning adults have recited some dreadfully dull poems to children in the past. Longfellow's "Ode to Childhood" quoted by our grandparents is not a poem *for* children, but a nostalgic view of an old man *about* childhood. Today's children are not cardboard-stiff "miniature adults," as boys and girls were often viewed during Victorian times. Poetry for children today opens up windows and doors to the soul with humor and whimsicality, as well as honest emotions, sometimes painfully expressed.

The umbrella of poetry encompasses many kinds of verse, such as narrative, humorous, and lyrical, and many forms, such as limericks, sonnets, free verse; poetry can come in various rhyme schemes or in unrhymed verse. "The Midnight Ride of Paul Revere," set in colonial America, represents a traditional narrative poem. Karen Hesse pushes the small confines of this form into a narrative poem-novel in her Newbery award–winning book *Out of the Dust*. Edward Lear's limericks and Lewis Carroll's nonsense verse from the past still tickle the funny bone. Contemporary poets Judith Viorst and Jack Prelutsky cause us to look humorously at today's world as kids view it. Viorst's poem "If I Was in Charge of the World" gives kids permission to gripe and add their own two cents through humorous solutions to everyday problems. Poetry has stepped out of the "stiff shirt" reputation it once had and become as comfortable as a pair of well-worn blue jeans.

But poetry lives in another part of our lives, too. It has the ability to touch the heart, sometimes even more deeply than novels or short stories. Eloise Greenfield's *Honey, I Love and Other Love Poems* wraps around the reader like a big hug. Who can remain unmoved by Joyce Carol Thomas's *Brown Honey in Broomwheat Tea*? Children express themselves in poetry, especially during times of trouble. One of my favorite books, *I Never Saw Another Butterfly,* was written by children held in a Nazi camp. Poetry can give people hope and strength and raise the spiritual longings in the listener.

This chapter is not intended to be a poetry textbook that outlines the many kinds of poetic forms, although I discuss acrostic poems, couplets, and quatrains. Instead, it offers a buffet of ideas and approaches from which to choose. Because of copyright restrictions, segments of popular poetry are not included, but I do share some of my own original verse. The purpose of this chapter is to introduce kids to poetry books and poetry activities in classroom and library settings.

Poetry Books

Adoff, Arnold. *Eats*. Lothrop, Lee & Shepard, 1979.

The word patterns in Adoff poems always catch kids off guard in a most appetizing way, and this volume serves a menu replete with vegetables cooked in a wok, a verse about learning to use chopsticks, and a poetic recipe about Grandma Ida's cookie crust for apple pie.

Alarcon, Francisco X. *Laughing Tomatoes and Other Spring Poems*. Children's Book Press, 1997.

The bilingual poems in this book by an award-winning Chicano poet celebrate tortillas and chilis, Cesar Chavez, and grandmother's songs. Bright graphic paintings and side notes add to the appeal of this cheerful collection.

Brenner, Barbara, compiler. *Voices, Poetry and Art from around the World*. National Geographic Society, 2000.

This book, arranged by the world's continents, includes poems about wagons from the American West, market women in Jamaica, songs from the looms of Nigeria, and dragons in China. Color photographs of art and other objects from all over the world accompany this rich, multicultural masterpiece of a book.

Fleischman, Paul. *Joyful Noise: Poems for Two Voices*. Illustrated by Eric Beddows. Harper and Row, 1988.

This Newbery Medal–winning book sets a new standard for children's poetry. The complex verses invite reading aloud by two voices that have practiced the timing and coordination of Fleischman's work. The rhythm and word choice match perfectly the dialogues among fireflies, grasshoppers, and other fascinating insects.

Greenfield, Eloise. *Honey, I Love and Other Love Poems*. Illustrated by Diane and Leo Dillon. Crowell, 1978.

The strong cadence of Greenfield's poetry rings out in this small volume of poems. Read this one aloud with attention to the rhythm when you share the verse with children you love.

Hopkins, Lee Bennett, compiler. *School Supplies, a Book of Poems*. Simon & Schuster, 1996.

One of the collections by Hopkins, a well-known poetry compiler, includes poems about pens, ballpoint pens, rubber-band bracelets, paperclips, and erasers. Hopkins always has an ear for good poetry, and this book includes the work of stellar poets such as Myra Cohn Livingston and Carl Sandburg.

Lesynski, Loris. *Nothing Beats a Pizza*. Annick Press, 2001.

Not all these poems are about pizza, but some of the best are! Wacky cartoon illustrations accompany verses about old, cold pizzas, Jack in the Beanstalk taking the role of a pizza delivery boy, and pizza-shaped clouds. The author provides a footnote to kids about writing their own poetry.

Prelutsky, Jack. *A Pizza the Size of the Sun*. Greenwillow, 1996.

This volume, illustrated by James Stevenson, is one among many by Prelutsky, a popular poet of humorous verse for children. The topics range from eyeballs for sale to bedraggled gerbils, and the poems are sure to stir laughter, quoting, and misquoting. Prelutsky's skill will inspire children to try writing their own poetry.

Stevenson, James. *Popcorn*. Greenwillow, 1998.

Similar to the author's Sweet Corn Poems, this small volume covers everyday topics from bakery goodies to a busted television in the woods. The title poem, "Popcorn," is a kind of metaphor for the small, snack-style poems that kids will want to read over and over.

Silverstein, Shel. *Where the Sidewalk Ends*. Harper Collins, 1974.

Young parents who remember this modern classic will want to introduce their own children to poems about a boa constrictor, Sarah Cynthia Stout's garbage, and Ickle Me Pickle Me. The invitation poem in this volume sets the tone for poetry's "flax-golden" magic found in his other poetry collections, too.

Thomas, Joyce Carol. *Brown Honey in Broomwheat Tea*. HarperCollins, 1993.

In this award-winning book, softly illustrated by Floyd Cooper's sepia-toned paintings, features family poems and lyrical verse that describe the bitter and sweet sides of growing up as a young African American girl.

Viorst, Judith. *If I Were in Charge of the World and Other Worries*. Atheneum, 1981.

Viorst has the ability to turn kids' worries into laughter in this charming book. Verses about going to the bathroom in the middle of the night, wishing you didn't have freckles, and being in charge of the world so you could declare chocolate sundaes were vegetables provide excellent models for kids to write their own "in charge of the world" poems.

Poetry Programs

Looking at the World Poetically: A Poetry Writing Workshop or Unit

Schools and public libraries can use this program in different ways. School media specialists can teach this unit cooperatively with language arts teachers in several sessions. Remember that before the actual writing begins, students need to be exposed to poems read aloud. They should also be given time to browse library shelves and read poems on their own. There are three parts to this program. Youth librarians in public settings may want to make poetry displays and advertise the program as an afternoon workshop lasting about two hours. If the workshop is successful, consider offering a follow-up session. School librarians may wish to use each part in a separate session.

Materials Needed

1. Objects to display around the room. (In the past, my colleagues and I have chosen a display on the theme "yellow" and used yellow objects for our display: yellow paper, splashes of yellow paint on white fabric, grapefruit, pitchers of lemonade, sunflowers, an egg yolk in a bowl, yellow sweat shirts or T-shirts, bananas, yellow book covers, yellow towels, yellow candles, yellow juggling balls, yellow pencils.)

2. Flip charts, whiteboards, or large art tablets

3. Paper and pencils or computers for student writers

4. A display of household objects, arranged as if they were in a specific room (Examples: a cozy chair, a floor lamp, a small table, a basket of magazines, a stack of library books scattered on the floor, writing tables and pencils)

Procedures

Part I: Poetry Webs

People create "idea webs" when they go through a brainstorming session to link words, ideas, themes, and concepts. Teachers use this process in planning their lessons and introduce webbing to students as they contribute diverse thoughts. Writers can use the same method in exploring words, phrases, and details that could be included in their writing. Follow these steps with young writers to help them start thinking poetically.

1. Tell the children that they will be thinking aloud together. Everyone's words and ideas—anything that pops into mind—is important. Set aside your "editor" today, and don't reject your own ideas, or those of the children. We all need lots of ideas to get our wheels spinning. The object in the end is to create a "group poem" with the ideas you have gathered.

2. Ask the children to look around the room, where you have placed a variety of objects of a certain color. In this case, the color is yellow. Ask what color is dominant in the room. (You could choose another focus, of course. Perhaps your display will have a sports equipment or snack food theme. Whatever you choose will be the "focus word.")

3. Tell children to write the focus word in the middle of their papers.

4. Ask participants to contribute ideas related to the focus word that pop into their heads. Play this part "by ear." Some children will mention objects in your display. Others will contribute phrases. Perhaps the "creative spirits" will come up with wild ideas. Accept them all, but with this cautionary note: violent, offensive, or abusive language will not be tolerated. Set this ground rule ahead of time.

5. Write down the words and phrases as children speak them. Think in terms of a spider web—the words will be "arranged" somewhat randomly. I try to group things in categories—for example, by writing book titles in the same area, descriptions close to objects, and so on—but for this kind of project, there are no rules. After the words are on the page, I draw lines relating ideas to one another. Don't be too literal as you do this part of the activity. Remember that you and the children are "brainstorming" a wild tangle of thoughts. At some point, you will add order to the chaos, but that comes later.

6. The following is an example of my own solo "brainstorm":

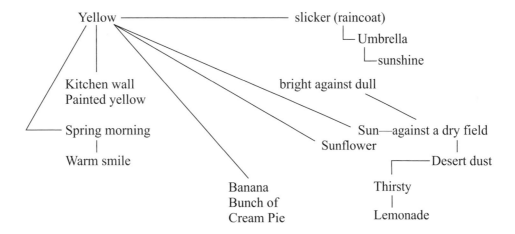

First, write down the words and ideas you come up with, then begin drawing the connecting lines. As you go through this process with your group, you'll cross words out, move them around, and revise. Then you'll draw lines between words; you'll choose to erase some of these later and add new ones. This process helps participants visualize the steps a poet might take in pulling together a variety of ideas for a poem. I created the following poem, "Sunflower in August," from my poetry web. Your poem will likely take a different slant.

Sunflower in August

Sunflower
Smiled at me
Through the dust
Of the dull dry desert
In my backyard
Yesterday afternoon.
August makes me
Feel all cracked and brown
And thirsty inside.
This morning
Tasted like sunflower lemonade
Cool on my tongue.

—Jan Irving

Take a break at this point if you think children need a rest. Serve lemonade.

Part II: Poetry Still Life

1. Point to the display of yellow objects again. Explain to children that artists arrange fruit, flowers, or other objects to draw or paint an artwork called a still life. Rather than creating a picture, you and the participants will arrange words into a "still life." You will build around the root word (in this example, I use yellow again). This time, concentrate on your senses. The web is built from the following pattern:

    Root Word:

    Tastes like:

    Sounds like:

    Smells like:

    Feels like:

2. The following example is my own poetry still life, based on the root word yellow:

    Root Word: Yellow

    Tastes like: butter, butterscotch pudding, egg yolk

    Sounds like: a whistle, a hum, a light laugh, twirling

    Smells like: lemons, roses, clean laundry, spring

    Feels like: a hug, a cotton sweater, hugging my dog

3. Now try putting some of the words and phrases together, adding lines as you feel the need.

Yellow

Smells like
Laundry fresh
From the sun outside
Tastes like egg yolk
Gooey on my plate
Feels like
Mama's hugs
At bedtime
And my holey
Old sweater.
Yellow makes me feel better than ever!

—Jan Irving

Part III: Poetry Sightings

Serious bird watchers view bird sites carefully and record their observations. They take along the proper tools, such as binoculars and notebooks. In like manner, invite young poets to go on a poetry sighting. Each young poet needs pencils and paper or a sketchbook. Take a nature walk, stopping at various times to write down details of what you see. In this exercise, you will not go outdoors but will write about a scene set up in a corner of the library.

1. Tell participants they will be recording details, phrases, even sentences about the display you have set up.

2. Remind participants to use sensory words and descriptive phrases. They might make their observations personal by evoking feelings or judgments about what they see.

3. Give the children about three to five minutes to make rough sketches or poetry drafts that they are willing to read aloud.

The following examples are my descriptions or poetry sightings of three displays on three days in February.

February 9

My room looks like a trash basket.
Socks rolled up under my bed.
Last week's test thrown in the closet with two pairs of white, blue, black, and mud splashed
Tennis shoes, old jeans, four shirts wrinkled, and my dog Spotty's half-chewed toy rabbit.
Sheets and blankets
Pulled up like a tent over my library books.
A tennis racket and flashlight hide out there, too.

February 10

Bathroom song
Sing me awake!
Soap fills my nose
Towels in place
Toothbrush standing in a cup
Waves hello—
Hey! I'm up!
Turn on the water
Here I go
Splash
Hum
Go, man, go!

February 11

Refrigerator raid
One hungry night,
What can I find?
What can I find
For my piece of bread?
Cheese spread gooey
Strawberry jam?
Yesterday's pizza and a chicken leg
Chocolate pie
One piece left
Whipped cream topping, yum
Really I shouldn't,
Or, maybe, I should . . .
Yes! I'll grab it and take
My fill,
Don't care now if my belly aches!

Ending the Workshop

Compile a poetry scrapbook of each person's poems. I suggest you photocopy the poetry so the participants can take home their creations, but the scrapbooks will become pleasant memories of the day. Take pictures of the writers to include in the scrapbook. Serve snacks at the end of the session if you wish. (If the focus word was yellow, cheddar cheese with golden yellow crackers and more lemonade would connect with the day's theme.)

Play with Words: A Writing and Acting Out Poetry Program

Many poems are meant to be read aloud, acted out, or performed on stage. The following program will take more than one session. In schools, use the procedure as your schedule allows. In public libraries, you might hold a one-hour choral reading program. The second session is devoted to writing poems or practicing the script given in this chapter. A third session is the public performance. If children submit their own poems, the librarian will select a group and turn these into a script so that children can read their own poems. To enter into the spirit of a play, select several children to take parts, reading different verses of the same poem. Intersperse these recitations with single participants reading one or more related poems.

Materials Needed

1. Books of poetry, including Mother Goose collections and other books, for example, Paul Fleischman's *Joyful Noise,* with copies of select poems and scripts you have prepared from poems (see example below)

2. Children who are comfortable reading aloud with loud voices and enthusiasm

3. Computers or pencil and paper for the writing portion of the program

4. Scripts for the final performance

I recommend that you have several adults available to help you work in small groups with the children.

Procedure

1. Give copies of a poem from *Joyful Noise* to the participants so they can see the arrangement of words on the page. Fleischman's clever use of columns to designate which reader is speaking and when both readers are speaking at the same time was a breakthrough for children's poems meant to be read aloud by two voices. Ask kids to read the poem silently. Then read the same poem aloud with another librarian or teacher with whom you have practiced. Fleischman's poetry takes a little practice to do justice to an oral reading. Children will benefit from hearing a poem read fluently before they attempt to try their "speaking wings."

2. Pass out copies of several poems from this book that you have selected for the group. Divide children into groups of two or four to practice reading aloud the poems. Each small group needs a leader to guide the participants and help them build confidence. At the end of "practice time," ask the duets if they would like to share their poem with everyone.

3. Give children another opportunity to read together with the "Mother Goose's Cats and Mice" script, which originally appeared in my book *Fanfares: Programs for Classrooms and Libraries* (Libraries Unlimited, 1990).

Mother Goose's Cats and Mice

Reader One: Hickory	**Reader Six:** The clock
Reader Two: Hickory	**Reader Five:** Tick tock
Reader Three: Dickory	**Reader Six:** Struck one
Reader Four: Dickory	**Reader One:** One
Reader One: Hickory	**Reader Six:** And down
Reader Three: Dickory	**Reader One:** Hickory
Reader Two: Hickory	**Reader Three:** Dickory
Reader Four: Dickory	**Reader Six:** He come
Reader Five: Dock	**Reader Two:** Hickory
Reader Six: The Mouse ran up	**Reader Four:** Dickory
Reader One: Hickory	**Reader One:** Hickory
Reader Three: Dickory	**Reader Three:** Dickory
Reader Six: The clock	**All:** Hickory Dickory Dock!
Reader Five: Dock!	**Reader Five:** STOP!

4. Open up volumes of Mother Goose rhymes and invite children to read the verses aloud as they play with the words as I have done in the preceding exercise.

5. At the end of this program, invite children to submit their original poems several days in advance of the next meeting. This will allow you to select poems and prepare a script for the performance "Play with Words."

6. As you select the poems, keep in mind how each one sounds when spoken aloud. Each poem can be read by one person, or it can be divided into several parts as in a play. A group of children might read several poems on a similar theme. Children may read the poems or memorize them. Consider using music or puppet play between the different parts of your "Play with Words."

7. The following made-up program will give you an idea of the flow of this activity. I have listed names for poems that might be written with names of readers as an example.

Play with Words: Program Draft for Your Planning

Host: Welcome, poetry lovers! We begin this play with words from poets young and old. The library kids in our community have written and practiced this play for you. To begin the program tonight, I'd like to recite this small poem.

> *A poem can take me inside myself*
> *Or out beyond our world. Such wealth!* (Stretch arms wide)
> *Inside I feel, sometimes, like a cat*
> *Tiptoeing, stalking, springing*
> *Like that!* (clap)
> *I play with words—*
> *Like tickle, fickle*
> *Pickle . . . squirm!* (Wiggle fingers)
> *I like to rhyme*
> *I like to dance*
> *I like to play*
> *With juicy words!*
> *Won't you join me* (Beckon to audience)
> *In this game*
> *Of light and laughter*
> *Wild and tame?*
> *Let go your stern*
> *And grouchy face*
> *Enter now*
> *The Poetry Place!* (Open arms wide)
>
> —Jan Irving

Now, the narrator-host introduces other poetry performers. For example:

- "A Sneaky Alligator," performed by Tad and Tom Valdez

- "I Had a Scary Dream," written and performed by Melissa Moore

- "Help!" written by Emily Andrews and performed by Emily with her friends Amy, Carrie, Courtney, and Sarah

- "Give Me a Break," written by Mary Fortelli and performed by Tom Judd, Sally Stump, and Mary Fortelli

- "Pickle Face," written and performed by Paul Porter
- "One Thought," written by Josea Huraldo and performed by Chad Gomez

When the performers have finished, the host closes the program.

Host: Our poems have ended. We hope you've enjoyed our play. Enjoy! Enjoy this happy day!

The following creative dramatics activity might be included in the previous program. Each character in this little play-in-verse represents a part of speech. Have children learn these brief lines. Ask each child to dress in a different color T-shirt or provide colored scarves for everyone. Add necklace signs (construction paper with string cords to wear around the neck) for each part of speech. I offer the following original script for your program.

The Parts of Speech: A Lively Poem for Your Enjoyment

Program Note: Have all parts of speech walk to the center of the stage area. All players bow. One by one, each part of speech steps forward to speak his or her lines and then steps back to the line. In the end, all the players bow.

Verb: I'm a verb,
A part of speech.
I dribble (act out)
I run (run in place)
I reach! (act out)
I'm a Verb (bow)
An active guy (wave one hand)
Hi! (wave other hand)

Adjective: I'm bold
Or shy (droop head)
I'm short (crouch)
Or tall (stand on tiptoes)
I really don't have to be here at all. (slump)
I'm called adjective (stand up with authority)
I describe you (point at audience)
Or Places you go
Busy New York
Or Things you use
Smelly dirty fork!

Noun: I'm the Noun
I name things
Jill, Jack
Bill, Mack
Frog
Dog
Cup
Pup
I'm important
As you can see
I know you will
Never forget me!

Conjunction: Hi! I'm not a big
Wig
I'm a helping hand
With words like "and"
"Or," " but,"
I can
Connect the nouns
You may have found
In this play
Oh, I'm conjunction
I almost forgot to say!

Pronoun: I'm also not as big
As my cousin Noun.
I'm called pronoun.
You can find me
In place of my cousin
With words like he, she,
Him or me
Use pronouns sparingly
Or I will confuse
The words you use.

Interjection: Stop! Whoa! Ouch!
I love attention!
I am interjection!

Adverb: Quietly, slowly
Take your place
I can control
The pace
Of your actions
And reactions
Often I end with
The letters "L Y"
I can tell you how to laugh
How sweetly to cry
My name is Adverb
I stick closely by
Adjective and Verb
I'm the very, very best
But, I seldom get to rest.

Preposition: Oh, don't forget
About me
I'm a tiny little part
Of every sentence.
Well, almost every
Sentence
If it's long.
Words like in of and around
Are prepositions

That's me
I help you get along.

All: (Each player steps forward and bows individually)
Verb
Adjective
Noun
Conjunction
Pronoun
Interjection
Adverb
Preposition
(All take hands)
Together we work
To organize your speech
Come take our gifts
Extend your reach!
Right? Write!

Idea Springboards: Activities to Develop

Poetry Chain

Try this variation on chain letters or e-mails. Compose one stanza of a poem. Write out the stanza five times and send it to five friends. In the instructions to this exercise, explain to the five recipients that they are invited to add a stanza to the verse and then pass it on to five friends. This can go on as long as you would like. You could ask each recipient to send another copy back to the person who sent the poem on so the progress of the poem can be enjoyed with each new addition.

School media specialists or youth librarians can arrange children in rows or circles to do this activity. You may want to develop electronic ways to develop this activity.

Funny Folks You Find in Poems:
A Writing Activity Built around Characters

Did you ever notice how Shel Silverstein creates many of his poems based on the personalities of people with funny names? Use this inspiration to write your own humorous poems. Begin making a list of silly names with clever descriptive words beginning with the same letter of the alphabet as the name. My list looks like this:

- Dreadful Dora

- Frantic Fred

- Greedy Gretchen

- Gabby George

- Creepy Clara

- Bumbling Bert

- Sassy Sarah

Next, write a little four-line verse (called a quatrain) with a simple rhyme scheme of lines two and four rhyming. You certainly can choose any other verse form or rhyming pattern you like, but I have found this is a fairly easy one to begin with. My completed poem follows.

Sassy Sarah
Tried to dance
But when she did
She lost her pants!

This is an everyday kind of poem, but it shows that playing with words can be an exercise to simply "start your poetic juices flowing."

You and Your Acrostics: A Writing Exercise for You and Your Friends

Kids like to describe themselves or someone they like. Acrostic poems have been written for many years and are not difficult to compose. These little poems look something like a game or a verse you could include in a valentine. Write the letters of a name vertically down a piece of paper. Next, add words and phrases to describe the person. This poem is about my friend Carol.

Caring
Always sharing
Reads all the time
One of a kind true friend
Loving lovely lady.

Poetry Murals: A Writing and Art Activity

Graffiti fills public walls and makes some of us cringe. Other "planned" graffiti on school or library walls inspire children to express themselves in artistically positive ways. Find a wall that needs decorating if you seek a more permanent project and give children paints and pens to write their own poems with illustrations. Stretch butcher paper on walls for a temporary display.

Kids will need a little practice on paper to refine their poems and draft their pictures. Their poems may be their own expressions, focused on a particular topic such as "Nature Verse" or "Tickle My Funny Bone," or they may be open-ended expressions. Acrostic poems may work for this project, or you can provide a topic such as "Classroom Crazies" or "I Love my Library."

These poems may be written on the paper, walls, or printed on long banners. (See Chapter 9, "Hooray for the USA" for ideas about how to work with banners.) The following shapes and poems could also serve as examples. Print them on brightly colored paper and place the poems in an attractive mosaic on a wall. Invite children to write their poems on posterboard and add pictures to celebrate poetry in your library or classroom.

My Very Best Friends Forever and Ever

I have a very long list of friends
Here they are at this moment—
If you want to know
My friends are
Janet with a smile
Carol who laughs
Kim and Sarah
Tim and Chad
Tom and Tommy
Ben and Sam
Let's see—there's me
I am Sam.

Fat

Do I look wide to you? I mean, am I the "F" word? Am I FAT? Oh no!
I thought I gained a little weight, just a little pudge around my waist.
But you think I look . . . Fat! Don't say it out loud
It makes me cringe
And feel bad somehow.
I thought I looked good in this new pair of jeans
But I guess you think I'll never look lean.
Oh, dear, will you like me however I am
Inside or outside, I'm really not mean!

Ouch!

Ouch! You just stepped on my face
I wasn't screaming
Or putting you
Down in your place.
I'm not nasty or bad
Like you think.
I may look tough
Sort of rough
But my heart's softer
Than that.
I hurt deep down here
Where the shadows walk about
Don't ask me to tell you
I'm too shy to shout!

7

Barrel of Fun

Books and Activities about Humor

What is funny? Cows saying "oink" instead of "moo"? Amelia Bedelia making a picture of the living-room drapes when she is told to "draw the drapes"? The line "What a funky smell!" in *The Stinky Cheese Man*? The emperor who takes off his clothes in the Hans Christian Andersen story "The Emperor's New Clothes"? Answer? It all depends!

Humor for children begins with simple word play and nonsense with a few pratfalls thrown in. For example, Bernard Most's *The Cow That Went Oink* begins with the lines, "There was once a cow that went OINK. The cows that went MOO laughed at the cow that went OINK." This obvious nonsense produces giggles from preschool-age children.

Humor evolves into puns for elementary students and develops into more sophisticated word play and allusion for older children. Children in early elementary school will laugh at Amelia Bedelia because they know more than the loveable, literal-minded maid. Beverly Clearly once wrote that children "enjoy feeling superior to their younger selves and are relieved to know they have grown." Children know the emperor who is tricked into buying new clothes (invisible to those unfit for their office) is a fool when he parades into town wearing nothing at all. Kids identify with Dav Pilkey's Captain Underpants because they can vicariously experience the fun of characters doing things they are not allowed to do in polite society.

What exactly do kids find funny? Although difficult to guess at times, experienced teachers and librarians know the elements and parameters of kids' humor. In our increasingly complex world, most children are quick to grasp more than we think they can. Television shows, popular media figures, and even current events shape adolescent humor. As much as ethnic humor and bawdy references offend sensitized people, this "forbidden" territory probably appeals even more to older children today because they like to test boundaries. Where does this leave teachers and librarians who select books to attract readers but also feel the responsibility of guiding kids?

In writing this chapter, I have searched for funny books and activities that will focus on the positive. My high school journalism teacher once told our school newspaper staff, "True humor is always kind." I have never forgotten that, and I think it bears repeating.

Laughter belongs in our libraries, schools, and lives. It has been part of the human experience since ancient times when the purposes of literature were to delight or amuse and to instruct. It helps us view the world in different ways. It gets us through difficult times. A poignant example of this philosophy can be seen in the film *Life Is Beautiful,* in which Roberto Benigni creates a make-believe comedic world for his son within the world of a Nazi concentration camp. On a lighter note, psychologists know that humor keeps the world in balance for us and prepares children to learn.

Educators who are concerned about justifying lessons through school standards can be assured that humor can always be counted on to develop thinking skills, no matter which subject is taught. Jon Scieszka and Lane Smith challenge children to problem solve through hilarious exaggeration in *Math Curse*. Debra Frasier's *Miss Alaineus, A Vocabulary Disaster* leads children to develop large vocabularies in a outrageously funny and touching story. *Scrambled States of the U.S.A.* transforms geography lessons into a humorously twisted tale of states changing locations. And how can science lessons stay dull when Miss Frizzle flies her magic school bus to teach children science?

This chapter introduces humorous books on all levels—grade level, reading level, as well as levels of understanding in terms of emotional development. Activities focus on categories such as word play, exaggeration, and situation humor, and on various genres of humor—riddles, jokes, fables, and expressions—cat out of the bag, off the wall, ants in your pants. When you engage children in these activities, they will have so much fun that they may not notice how much they are learning in the process.

Humor Books

Because humor is so popular with young people, hundreds of talented authors have created a vast world of delightful novels, picture books, poetry collections, as well as volumes of riddles and jokes. This list does not even begin to scratch the surface if folktales, fables, and other books combining humor are included. The list that follows is highly selective, with representative books to introduce this topic.

Brown, Marc. *Arthur's Chicken Pox*. Little, Brown and Company, 1994 (picture book).

Brown's loveable character Arthur catches chicken pox in this particular story, but sister D.W. becomes jealous of all the attention her brother receives. She gloats that Arthur will have to stay home when the family goes off to the circus only to have the tables turned on her. Arthur gets well in time for the big event, but D.W. catches her own case of chicken pox just as the family is ready to go. Brown's many Arthur tales have captured a growing audience of devoted readers, and the quality of the writing remains high in every book, unlike other multiple-book series.

Fleischman, Sid. *McBroom Tells a Lie*. Little, Brown and Company, 1976 (novel).

Fleischman's short tall tales are perfect fare for second- and third-grade readers who have recently moved from picture books into longer fiction. In this story, Farmer McBroom makes a bet with his obnoxious neighbor Heck Jones to keep the heckler off of his property. Heck's request that McBroom grow a crop of tomatoes overnight during a dust storm seems like an impossible task, but the eleven McBroom children's invention of a Popcornmobile saves the day. Other McBroom tales include *McBroom Tells the Truth, McBroom the Rainmaker,* and *McBroom's Ghost.*

Frasier, Debra. *Miss Alaineus, A Vocabulary Disaster*. Harcourt, 2000 (picture book).

Because Sage missed school on Vocabulary Day, she has to get the words over the telephone from a friend. She misunderstands one of the words and ends up with a far different spelling and meaning for "miscellaneous." Sage decides the word must be spelled "Miss Alaineus" and attaches a very unusual definition to the word. The whole class collapses into laughter, thus humiliating poor Sage. In the end, she turns her mistake into a winning solution. She makes a prize-winning costume for the Annual Vocabulary Parade. The word play and whole concept of a vocabulary parade are so much fun that students will want to engage in this activity, too.

Hurwitz, Johanna. *Aldo Peanut Butter*. Morrow Junior, 1990 (novel).

When Aldo Sossi receives five dogs for his birthday, his mother balks at keeping more than one. They compromise at two dogs, one brown mutt and one white mutt, whom Aldo names "Peanut" and "Butter." Soon after the dogs join the family, both Mom and Dad are called away from home. The Sossi kids become embroiled in all kinds of crazy canine problems described in Hurwitz's typically lighthearted, down-to-earth style. Other Aldo books by the author include *Aldo Applesauce* and *Aldo Ice Cream.*

Laden, Nina. *Roberto the Insect Architect*. Chronicle, 2000 (picture book).

The sophisticated word play in Laden's story involves a termite named Roberto who dreams of becoming an architect. No one in the big city will pay attention to him, but the hardworking insect turns a junkyard into a block of unique houses that his clients love. Fly receives a house, turning her into a house fly, Carpenter Ant moves into a workshop, and Ladybug moves into a fireproof dwelling. Each idiomatic expression is printed in bold type, and the collage illustrations made from wood veneers, magazines, and blueprints are likely to inspire young writers to write their own humorous stories.

Lobel, Arnold. *Fables*. Harper and Row, 1980 (fable/folktale).

A Caldecott Honor Book, this modern fable collection includes twenty stories about the peccadilloes and idiosyncrasies of animals. A crocodile obsessed with order becomes ill looking at the tangle in a real garden and prefers the perfectly ordered flowers on his wallpaper. Camel is convinced she is a marvelous dancer, and Madame Rhinoceros believes people admire her dress. Instead, both animals are victims of grand delusions. Children will enjoy the stories and morals at the end. This is a good resource for urging children to create their own modern fables

Manes, Stephen. *Chocolate-Covered Ants*. Scholastic, 1990 (novel).

Here's another food story on the slightly gross side, guaranteed to delight kids, especially boys in the middle elementary grades. Adam receives an ant farm from his aunt for his birthday, but he has to wait for the shipment of ants to get the fun started. Adam and his brother Max then get all mixed up into making chocolate-covered ants that people will want to eat. The book literally explodes with zany humor.

Meddaugh, Susan. *Martha Speaks*. Houghton Mifflin, 1992 (picture book).

The day Helen feeds vegetable soup to her dog, Martha, the letters in the soup go to the dog's brain instead of her stomach. At first Helen's family is amused by the dog's ability to carry on conversations, telling them just what is on her mind. As the story proceeds, Martha's blunt talk creates embarrassing situations that young readers will love, for they, too, have been guilty of such blunders. Martha herself realizes she has become a pest, so she stops eating the soup that has fueled her talking. Only when Martha alerts the police during a house burglary is the faithful dog forgiven. Meddaugh's sequels to this book continue the hilarious tales about Martha.

Numeroff, Laura. *If You Give a Pig a Pancake*. Laura Geringer/HarperCollins, 1998 (picture book).

One of this author's popular series that began with *If You Give a Mouse a Cookie* continues the same humorous sequence of events that happens by a seemingly innocent act. The first consequences may be reasonably logical (i.e., If you give a pig a pancake, she will want syrup to go with it), but the humorous exaggeration goes on to the pig taking a bubble bath, dancing in tap shoes, and building a tree house. Use this book as a model for students telling their own exaggerated stories based on a single open-ended statement.

Palatini, Margie. *Piggie Pie!* Clarion, 1995 (picture book).

Gritch the Witch wakes up hungry for a tasty Piggie Pie, but she needs eight plump pigs to complete the recipe. Checking the yellow pages of the phone book, the witch finds a listing for Old MacDonald's farm, where she tries to lure the pigs. In the end, Gritch gives up, but she invites a skinny old wolf to her house again. Palatini's clever illustrations reveal the little piggies dressed in a variety of disguises, and young readers will enjoy each pig trick that fools Gritch.

Parish, Peggy. *Teach Us, Amelia Bedelia*. Scholastic, 1977 (picture book).

In this tale the literal-minded, loveable housemaid becomes a substitute teacher who tries to follow the regular teacher's list. Amelia ends up calling a roll in a student's lunchbox, planting light bulbs during science class, and concocting taffy apples to make amends for her literal-minded mistakes. The obviously goofy behavior of this character appeals to elementary-age students who know more than the dim-witted Amelia Bedelia.

Pinkwater, Daniel. *The Magic Pretzel.* Aladdin Paperbacks, 2000 (novel).

Norman and his friends become members of the Werewolf Club sponsored by their teacher, Mr. Talbot. When Mr. Talbot reveals his identity as a cross between a man and a wolf, the children (also turned into werewolf cubs) try to get the magic pretzel to break the werewolf curse. Typically outlandish Pinkwater humor will win the hearts of those with an offbeat sense of humor. This book is the first in the Werewolf Club series.

Rockwell, Thomas. *How to Eat Fried Worms.* Franklin Watts, 1973 (novel).

Billy makes a $50 bet that he can eat fifteen worms. The chapters build worm-by-worm with hilarious results that have kept kids laughing for thirty years. This "classic" is still the model for slightly gross, good-natured humor and a "must read" for elementary students.

Schwartz, Alvin. *Whoppers, Tall Tales and Other Lies.* Harper and Row, 1975 (fable/folktale).

Schwartz's compilation of short stories taken from the American folklore tradition explores a variety of topics, all told as lies or tall tales. Categories include the weather, ordinary people, and extraordinary wonders. These tales will help children explore the imagination and understand the nature of exaggeration in humor. Notes and sources for the tales will supply information for teachers to extend this rich collection by one of America's best compilers of folklore for children.

Scieszka, Jon. *Knight of the Kitchen Table.* Viking, 1991 (novel).

In this Time Warp trio tale, Joe receives "the book" from his magician uncle. Upon opening the book, Joe and his friends become caught up in the world of Camelot. There they meet knights and dragons in a time-warped adventure that delights second-grade boys (and girls), who receive a touch of history laced with outrageous fun.

Scieszka, Jon, and Lane Smith. *Squids Will Be Squids.* Viking, 1998 (fable/folktale).

The author-illustrator team that created a body of wacky picture books encourages young readers to make their own fables by thinking like Aesop, turning people into animals, and adding a moral. Squids are party poopers; Little Walrus tells the painful truth when he tells the *whole* truth; and Shark, Wasp, and Bacteria can't understand why no one wants to eat lunch with them. The fables are so funny, and the morals so silly, that students will beg for more.

Shannon, David. *A Bad Case of the Stripes.* Blue Sky/Scholastic, 1998 (picture book).

Camille Cream resists eating lima beans even though she likes them. As a result, she wakes up with brightly colored stripes on her face. The doctor gives her an ointment, but the next day Camille's face breaks out in red and white stripes with blue stars. Each day, the girl is the victim of wilder and wilder facial decorations. No expert seems to be able to solve Camille's growing problems until a sweet old woman brings a bag of beans to the Cream's house. When Camille eats the beans, she reverts to her own self, proving that one should always be true to their own nature.

Yolen, Jane. *A Sip of Aesop.* Blue Sky, Scholastic, 1994 (fable/folktale).

Prolific author Yolen chooses about a dozen Aesop fables to retell in rhyme, adding to the humor and hilarity of the original tales.

Humor Programs

Off the Wall and Out of the Bag—A Humor Writing Workshop or Lessons

The writing exercises and activities described here fill several class periods. In public libraries, all the activities can be completed in a workshop lasting about two hours. When you advertise the program in the public library, ask children to bring an original joke and a riddle that they have written. Each joke and riddle should be written on separate index cards. These are the "tickets" for admission to the workshop.

Materials Needed

1. A roll of brown wrapping paper or butcher paper

2. Several boxes of medium-sized colored markers

3. Lined paper and pencils or computers for student writers

4. Tables and chairs for young writers

5. Sweet snacks such as brownies, cookies, and sheet cake squares; fruit beverages in small cartons

6. A copy of Scieszka's *Squids Will Be Squids* or Lobel's *Fables,* and other humor books.

Procedure

1. Before children come to the program, stretch long horizontal lengths of plain paper, such as butcher paper or brown wrapping paper, across a wall or on several walls.

2. Prepare a display of humorous books. Your display might include joke and riddle books as well as some of the picture books and fables listed in this chapter's bibliography.

3. Set up tables with paper, pencils, and markers.

4. Librarian and adult or high school helpers might dress in silly clothes. Perhaps the leader will want to wear a jester's hat and carry a wand to urge the audience to clap or cheer after each joke is read aloud.

5. Begin the program by asking kids to read aloud the jokes and riddles they have brought. Have extra jokes written on cards for those children who didn't remember to bring a joke or riddle. Leader prompts kids to laugh, clap, or cheer after each joke is read.

Activity: Off the Wall Writing

1. Read one of the short humorous tales found in *Squids Will Be Squids* or a fable from Lobel's *Fables.* You may also choose a humorous poem from the bibliography in Chapter 6 of this book.

2. Explain the expression "off the wall" to the group. This phrase refers to humor that is against the grain or funny because it goes beyond the norm.

3. Invite kids to go to the wall and write jokes, funny graffiti, cartoons, or quotes from favorite stories on the paper murals. Tell them this is an "OK" place to write graffiti. Set ground rules about "acceptable" humor (no abusive language or harmful or obscene words), then watch the creativity come out! See a few ideas in the boxes that follow. These exaggerations were inspired by the book *Whoppers*, a collection of American folklore.

I know a woman
who is so skinny
that . . .
you can see
her back and
front at the
same time.

I know another
woman who is
so skinny
she can walk
through the
eye of a needle.

And I know a man
who is so tall
that the rain
hits his head
fifteen minutes
before it
touches
the ground.

Corny

One summer it got so hot in Kansas
That the corn grew twenty feet tall.
And that's not all!
The corn popped in the field.
The cows thought it was snow!
So . . . they started shivering
and shivering
until they made ice cold vanilla shakes instead of milk!

Activity: Out of the Bag

1. Tell children that the expressions that make no literal sense but take on another meaning are called "idioms." For example, to say you are "in a pickle" does not really mean you are inside a pickle, but that you are in a difficult situation.

2. Write out the following expressions on index cards with the beginning of a story for children to finish. You can consult dictionaries of clichés and idioms in the library for more expressions.

Cat Got Your Tongue

Chad is a chatty kid. He talks all the time and drives his class-mates crazy. His teacher sends him to the principal's office because he will not stop talking. Kids plug their ears to blot out his talking. Finally, his pet cat grabs Chad's tongue and won't let go of it until . . .

Tell the full story in your own words and finish it.

Butterflies in the Stomach

Emma the pet goat wasn't hungry anymore—not after she ate all the flowers in Miss Daisy's garden. Five minutes later, Emma became worried that she may have eaten more than just the flowers. Her stomach began to jump and jitter and feel all quivery inside. Emma thought she might have eaten the butterflies that were flying around the garden.

Tell this story in your own words, and create your own ending.

Activity: Comeuppance Comedy

1. Explain to children that one kind of humor makes fun of a character who deserves a "comeup-pance," or deserved punishment. Big Anthony in Tomie dePaola's *Strega Nona* makes a magic pasta pot cook too much pasta. His comeuppance is to eat the excess pasta. Echo, the character in Greek mythology, pines too long for the self-seeking Narcissus, now turned into a flower. She loses her voice, only able to repeat what other people say.

2. Distribute index cards with these story starters that involve "Comeuppance Comedy."

The Sneaker Kid

The Sneaker Kid wants to win the spring school race so much that he runs to the sneaker store at the mall. He insists on getting the best pair of super snapper sneakers. He gets grabby—way too grabby. He pulls the box away from the saleswoman and jams the sneakers onto his fat feet. Once he puts on the sneakers, he can't stop running. He runs out of the mall without paying. He runs through a traffic jam. He runs onto a racetrack of dogs, who run after him.

What happens next? Tell the story in your own words and add an ending.

The Gooey Gluey Chocolate Bar

Brown Elementary School Principal Stuffit eats chocolate bars all day. Every day he talks to every classroom as he pops chocolate balls and chocolate bars into his fat face. He jingles the coins in his pockets. He talks and he eats. He makes the kids crazy. Billy the Wild Kid dares to do what every kid dreams of doing—Billy puts a chocolate bar in the library window until it becomes really gooey and gluey. Then he slips the chocolate bar, smeared with glue, into the principal's pocket. When Stuffit sticks his hand inside the pocket . . .

Finish the story in your own words to come up with a comeuppance ending.

Bargain Mart Pet Shop

Bargain Mart announces that their "unusual pets" are on sale for 90 percent off. The stingiest bargain shoppers line up outside the shop to buy these pets. The parakeets seem especially talky. The cats are cross eyed. The dogs have chewed-off ears. But a bargain is a bargain, so the customers buy up all these unusual pets. When the parakeets come home, the owners become afraid of what the birds say. The cats don't speak at all, but their behavior is very odd, and the dogs always have something in their mouths.

Tell the whole story with a comeuppance ending.

Humor on Stage: A Drama Workshop on Humor

Stage this event in the public library as an impromptu humorous drama workshop. Some of the activities can be used in both school libraries or classrooms.

Materials Needed

1. Scripts, paper, and pencils

2. Displays of humorous books selected from this chapter's bibliography

3. Video camera

4. Popcorn snacks

Procedure

1. Warm up the children with these little exercises. Ask for volunteers to perform the mimes.

2. Write the following actions on index cards to give to each volunteer. (Write out some of your own silly mimes to add to the three examples I have prepared for you.)

3. Give the children about one minute to think through what to mime. Then ask each kid to perform their mime for the audience. Limit the audience to three guesses to determine what action is being performed.

4. Give each participant a container of silly putty or a slinky as an award for their performance.

Act this out for the audience:

You wake up one morning and jump out of bed.
Your jump is much higher than you thought you could jump.
You look down at your feet.
Somehow your feet have been replaced by big springs.

Act out this scene and add details of your own:

You look down on the street. What is that dirty pink gob?
You look closer and closer, until you discover the gob is a hunk of
    old bubblegum.
Only problem? It gets stuck on your nose.

You are walking around a swamp.
Everything seems very quiet until you sense something is following you.
You turn around, but the only thing behind you is a frog. A big ugly frog.
You turn back around.
Suddenly the frog is talking to you and sounds like your best friend.
You turn around again to speak to your friend, but realize your friend's
    voice comes out of the mouth of the frog.

Act out what happens next.

The Fable Cable

Capitalize on the popularity of cable networks that offer many special interest shows. Call on three or four volunteers to work with small groups of children who will be acting out or reading scripts based on their favorite fables. You can prepare the scripts ahead of time or let children extemporaneously act out a fable the volunteer reads to the group.

Materials Needed

1. Collections of fables such as those mentioned in this section

2. Writing supplies: pencils, paper, or word processors

Procedure

1. When children arrive, tell them that today they will be participating in a special cable show being videotaped for future viewing. The show is called *The Fable Cable*.

2. Divide children into three or four small groups to prepare and practice their scripts with the volunteers.

3. Suggested fables for this activity include the following selections from three books listed in the bibliography: *Fables* by Lobel, *Squids Will Be Squids* by Scieszka, and *A Sip of Aesop* by Yolen. Look for other versions of the fables you choose in your library collection, and then write your own version.

Fables to Use

"The Bad Kangaroo" (Lobel, *Fables*)
"The Boy Who Cried Wolf" (Yolen, *A Sip of Aesop*)
"The Frogs at the Rainbow's End" (Lobel, *Fables*)
"The Grasshopper and the Ants" (Yolen, *A Sip of Aesop*)
"Shark, Wasp and Bacteria" (Scieszka, *Squids Will Be Squids*)
"Slugs Will Be Slugs" (Scieszka, *Squids Will Be Squids*))

4. After planning and practice time (about twenty-five to thirty minutes), the leader announces the show with dialogue something like this:

Narrator: Good afternoon comedy fans! Today we bring you our first episode on "The Fable Cable." Frogs, ants, slugs, and bacteria will be featured in these fables guaranteed to make you think and cause you to laugh. After our actors take their places, we will begin with the performance of "The Bad Kangaroo." I will announce each fable. Please applaud after each and every performance.

5. One of the volunteers can tape the entire show. Each group performs in the order you determine. At the end of the show, the narrator should sign off by thanking the "viewers who have tuned into "The Fable Cable." (Note: When performing and taping copyrighted material, be sure to check copyright restrictions that may apply.)

6. Serve popcorn snacks.

Idea Springboards: Activities to Develop

Joke Jar Contest

Place a gallon-sized jar on the service desk in the library and stack small colored squares of paper next to it for children to write out their own jokes. Visual jokes, cartoons, and narratives are all acceptable. Make a slot in the top of the jar for kids to insert their entries. Use this format to remind children to sign each entry.

Title of Joke:

The Joke:

Your Name:

Phone Number:

Humor in Your Hand Card Game

Make your own card game by making four sets of identical cards, each with the title of a humorous book on the back and a similar design on the front. Make ten "sets" using the title of a humorous book listed in this chapter's bibliography. After you have printed the cards, let the children play with them using their own rules or using rules similar to those of popular game of Authors.

Keen Jeans Booktalkers

Books to Booktalk and Teaching Kids to Become Booktalkers

After kids begin to read "well enough" on their own (somewhere around third or fourth grade), we stop reading to them and sharing our enthusiasm for the "worth it" books. These kids, mired down in homework assignments, escape into the world of computer games, media "fixes," and active social lives. If they read at all for pleasure, many grab the latest Garfield cartoon collection or another comic that appeals only to the fast-forward pace of their lives. Do we fill library shelves with only the "popular titles"? Are we booksellers or book guides? What can caring parents, teachers, and librarians do to nudge kids over the reading wasteland of too many junk books to the place where books become a continuing source of enjoyment, enlightenment, and a better education?

Look back to the bookmarks in Chapter 1 of this book to remind you of tricky ways to capture readers. Keep in mind that independent readers in middle to upper elementary grades are a "hard sell." They may already consider themselves "too cool" to read. So those of us who love the excitement of classic and newly published books need to be booksellers. We must pull out all of the "tricks of the trade" to grab the attention of readers in the older elementary school grades. But how exactly can we do that?

First, we can make the "look of books" attractive, just as bookstores have learned to do to capture sales. Shabby books and messy shelves do not attract readers. Weed those collections!

Next, arrange books in eye-catching displays.

Then get to the heart of the matter. Talk up those books! Don't just do booktalk for kids. Teach *kids* how to booktalk. Replace the dreaded old book report. Teach kids how to sell books to other kids.

Think about the added benefits of passing on the skill of doing booktalks. You will be teaching children to focus on the main action and the most appealing features of the books they read. You will end that boring recitation of kids droning on about "This happened. Blah, blah, blah. Then this happened. Blah, blah, blah." No one enjoys hearing "Blah, blah, blah." You will help students become effective speakers who want to capture the attention of the audience.

In case you have not been in the practice of doing booktalks, remember that they are simply little book advertisements. Booktalks can be as brief as a minute or two or as lengthy as ten to fifteen minutes. There aren't hard-and-fast rules for booktalking, except that you never tell the ending. I like to mention the title of the book and author several times. Tell just enough about the story to capture the attention of young readers. Be enthusiastic, but don't oversell, especially among this age group, which identifies with being "cool."

Although this chapter will help you, the professional, sharpen your booktalking skills, it is mostly intended as a method to teach kids how to do their own booktalks.

You can make the booktalk program sound like "big stuff" to kids by providing incentives: book bags, cool folders with notebooks and jazzy pencils, and the promise that they will not have to write book reports. Yea! Just read books and talk about them to your friends. This is called booktalking, and everyone will want to be part of your BNBR (Booktalk Not Book Report) group.

In a public library, begin a Keen Jeans Book Club. Keen Jeaners will make jazzy book bags, then go on to read books, learn how to booktalk, and finally discuss books with one another. The keen jeans bag described in this chapter is a perfect display item, and it can be used to hold books kids will want to check out. See the following full-scale program description for other book-related activities to use with this age group.

This chapter's bibliography will list appealing books for booktalks. Other resources about the skill of booktalking appear in the resource bibliography at the back of this book.

Books for Booktalks

Avi. *Nothing but the Truth*. Orchard Books, 1991 (libraries and books).
This avant-garde novel tells Phillip Malloy's story of getting in trouble for defiantly humming the National Anthem in class. A communitywide battle begins over the issue of First Amendment rights. The story is told through news articles, interviews, and announcements rather than in straight narrative.

Babbitt, Natalie. *Tuck Everlasting*. Farrar, Straus & Giroux, 1975 (fantasy, thought-provoker).
The recent film has introduced this classic fantasy about ten-year-old Winnie Foster who meets a strange boy in the woods, who drinks from a special pool of water. She learns from his family about the secret water that brings everlasting life to those who drink from it, and she begins to examine her own thoughts about this perplexing situation.

Baker, E. D. *The Frog Princess*. Bloomsbury Children's Books, 2002 (frogs/toads).
Esmeralda, an unlikely princess, meets a frog named Eadric. Her kiss, which is intended to turn the frog back into a prince, fails. Instead, it turns Esmeralda into a frog, too. The botched magic works itself out by the end, but not until the two frogs experience many humorous adventures.

Cleary, Betsy. *Dear Mr. Henshaw*. Morrow, 1983 (diary).
Leigh Botts hates the class assignment that instructs kids to write to their favorite author. But in satisfying the assignment, Leigh becomes a steady correspondent with Mr. Henshaw. He also begins to keep a diary to work through his own problems concerning his parents' divorce and getting along with his classmates. This Newbery Award–winning book captures the hearts of readers who may also feel alone.

Cole, Brock. *The Goats*. Farrar, Straus & Giroux, 1987 (kids on their own, challenges).
Two kids at a summer camp become the goats who are seriously taunted by the other campers. After they are stripped of clothes and dignity, the kids learn to survive and triumph in the end.

Conford, Ellen. *The Frog Princess of Pelham*. Little, Brown & Company, 1997 (fantasy, frogs/toads).
Chandler, a feisty orphan who lives with Cousin Horaces, manages not to go to summer camp. Instead, she stays at home, receives a kiss from Danny, a cute boy she likes, and magically turns into a frog. Chandler and Danny undergo hilarious adventures throughout the book.

Coville, Bruce. *Jennifer Murdley's Toad*. Harcourt, Brace, Jovanovich, 1992 (fantasy, frogs/toads).

Jennifer Murdley buys a talking toad from the Magic Shop, but the pet only adds to her troubles. When the toad turns Jennifer's best friend into a toad, a plague of toad transformations begin.

Creech, Sharon. *Love That Dog*. Joanna Cotler Books/HarperCollins, 2001 (diary).

Jack doesn't like poetry at all, but when he learns to express his thoughts in poetry written for his teacher, he changes his mind. This unusual book is told both in diary form and in poetry.

Curtis, Christopher Paul. *Bud, Not Buddy*. Delacorte, 1999 (kids on their own).

Ten-year-old Buddy runs away from an orphanage during the Great Depression. He is going to Chicago to find his long lost father. Because Buddy thinks his dad is a musician, he gets to know jazz musicians in the city. His quest ends in a surprise that will intrigue young readers.

Dahl, Roald. *James and the Giant Peach*. Knopf, 1961 (fantasy).

When young James Trotter is orphaned, he goes to live with two despicable aunts. All is not lost, because James receives magic crystals from an old man. The crystals accidentally spill on the aunts' peach tree, making it grow giant fruit. James then crawls inside a peach where fantastic adventures happen.

Hesse, Karen. *Out of the Dust*. Scholastic, 1997 (challenges).

Set in the Oklahoma Dust Bowl during the Great Depression, Billie Jo must learn to forgive her father for contributing to the death of her mother. This Newbery Award book tells this emotionally wrought story entirely through poetry. Outstanding writing and a gripping story win the hearts of readers of all ages.

Ibbotson, Eva. *The Secret of Platform 13*. Dutton, 1998 (fantasy).

A baby prince is kidnapped from his royal parents on Platform 13 in an old Tube station in London. Nine years later, a party of weird creatures from the island where the prince was born rescue him from the Trottle family. Harry Potter fans will enjoy this book, which is also reminiscent of Roald Dahl's books.

LaFaye, A. *The Year of the Sawdust Man*. Simon & Schuster, 1998 (challenges).

Nissa, abandoned by her "free spirit" Mama, clings to her father as she tries to sort out the reasons her mother ran away. This coming of age story set in rural Louisiana during the Depression will encourage young people who feel alone to find courage and strength.

Lowry, Lois. *The Giver*. Houghton Mifflin, 1993 (thought-provoker).

Jonas, the young hero of this complex and haunting novel set in a future time, begins to understand the terrible truth of his society. He is given a special role—he will be the receiver of all memories from an old man called the Giver. People who read this Newbery Award book will be challenged to examine their own values.

Lowry, Lois. *Number the Stars*. Houghton, 1989 (challenges, thought provoker).

This Newbery Award book set in occupied Denmark during World War II describes a young Jewish girl's fears. She is taken into the home of a non-Jewish family to escape Nazi persecution. This is a tense story with historical importance that will cause readers to examine their own consciences.

Paterson, Katherine. *The Same Stuff as Stars*. Clarion Books, 2000 (kids on their own).

Angel Morgan and her brother Bernie are driven to their great-grandma's shack, where their mother deserts them. Dad is in jail. But Angel learns to rise above the grim circumstances through the gentle guidance of an eccentric man who teaches her to learn about stars and the wonders of the sky.

Paulsen, Gary. *Hatchet*. Bradbury, 1987 (kids on their own).

When the pilot of a two-passenger plane has a fatal heart attack, the boy flying with him manages to land it. He learns to survive the wilderness by developing his own skills with the assistance of a hatchet left on the crashed plane.

Spinelli, Jerry. *The Library Card.* Scholastic, 1997 (library/books).

The amazing stories in this book have common elements. They are all about library cards and books. Library cards lead kids into unusual adventures, sometimes by literally pulling them into the fantasy world of a book, other times by presenting surrealistic circumstances. A homeless kid finds peace in the library, and a lonely girl finds happiness by riding in a bookmobile every day.

Booktalk Programs and Workshops

Booktalks, Not Book Reports—A Booktalk Program for Schools

As the introduction to this chapter suggests, this program replaces the boring old book report with today's more active approach, booktalking. The instructions cover three sessions, but this program is intended to be an ongoing one, in which classroom teachers and media specialists work together to help kids find good books and learn how to share them with classmates. This dynamic activity will help kids focus on the main plot and theme of books, and it will sharpen oral language skills.

Materials Needed

1. Books! Beef up your library collections. Ask for extra funds from parent groups and community organizations when you begin this program

2. Index cards, notebooks, and pencils for students

3. Jean vests or T-shirts that promote reading for kids, if possible (There are many produced commercially that can be purchased.)

4. Plastic or cloth book bags, either purchased or made, such as the jeans bags described in the next program for the Keen Jeans Book Club

Procedure

1. In preparation for a booktalk program, you must first read a lot of books yourself. Remember that librarians and teachers need to stay ahead of children by reading "professionally." This means you should at least skim, or spot read the books. Read first and last chapters, then read through the rest of the book quickly until you understand what is happening.

2. Document your reading. Keep note cards or journals or some kind of database as you read. Note title, author, main characters, plot line, and a "grabber" such as a telling line or dramatic moment. You're now "reading professionally."

3. Choose one to four books to "booktalk" to your student booktalkers-to-be.

4. Read these books carefully. Look back at the initial notes you made about the book. Find important passages in the book that you may want to quote.

5. Try to summarize the main point of the story in your own words. The tone should be friendly and inviting, not formal. Think of a detail or two that might make this book "come alive" for an audience—for example, a quirky character, a fascinating setting, or an intriguing plot. Plan a catchy beginning and ending to your booktalk. Remember, don't tell the ending!

6. Practice your booktalk aloud several times.

7. If you plan to introduce several books on a common theme, think about topics your students might enjoy or books that you think need special promotion.

8.   Make an attractive display of books such as those listed in the earlier bibliography of this chapter. Choose books with attractive and colorful covers.

9.   Invite students to the first session of your program "BNBR—Booktalks Not Book Reports."

10.   Students receive a folder or bag with index cards, notebook, pencils, and a shirt if you can afford them.

11.   Do your own booktalks. Have students choose a book to read and booktalk at the next session.

12.   Give out photocopies of the booktalking bookmark provided later in this section.

13.   At the second meeting, students should have read their books and begun a draft of the booktalk.

14.   Discuss student progress and ask for volunteers to practice the rough booktalk. Have them practice in pairs.

15.   By the third session, students should be able to jump into their booktalks given aloud to one another.

16.   The sessions that follow repeat the same procedure just described and add discussion about books and lessons from teachers and media specialists about various literature genres—poetry, historical fiction, fantasy, biographies, and so on.

17.   At the end of a school quarter, you might want to compile a booktalk notebook or file of index cards students have submitted for others to consult when they look for books to read.

Note: The "How to Booktalk" Bookmark may be reproduced for students. The sample booktalks I have prepared give you examples of a theme program appropriate for a school setting.

BNBR Booktalkers Tip Sheet

1. Read through your book.

2. On your index card, write down the title, author, and main story line in two or three sentences.

3. List the main characters.

4. Write down the main theme or idea of the book.

5. Write down a quote from the book or the page number where you can find the quote. Put a Post-it note in the book where the quote appears.

6. Think of a catchy beginning and ending. Remember—don't tell the ending.

7. Practice your booktalk from the notes you have made.

8. If you wish, write out the entire booktalk on another index card.

9. Speak loudly, slowly, and distinctly.

10. Add enthusiasm. Remember you are selling the book!

The following booktalks are samples of how you can sell books to other readers. They may be adapted and used for your own booktalks, but the most effective booktalks are those you create yourself.

Books, Truth, and Library Cards: A Booktalk Program

Did you ever think a library card was magic? Is truth scary? Listen to find out!

Nothing but the Truth by Avi
Orchard Books, 1991.

Phillip Malloy is a jock. He does all right in most of his classes, but he can't seem to get along in English. When he gets a D on his report card, Coach Jamison will not let him participate in track until he shapes up. Instead of shaping up, Phillip dares his homeroom teacher, who just happens to be his English teacher, to defy him.

One morning when the National Anthem is played over the intercom, the class is respectfully quiet except for Phillip, who starts humming the song. "Is that you, Phillip?" Phillip tells her he is just humming. Miss Narwin tells him to stop. Phillip does not stop. Miss Narwin tells him again to stop. Phillip does not.

From that moment on, a dreadful battle begins. Phillip's defiance and Miss Narwin's attempt to take control are blown out of proportion. Clearly Phillip has crossed a line, but his parents and the townspeople, principal, and school board see the truth differently. Should Phillip be expelled for singing or humming a patriotic song? Perhaps his teacher is guilty of stifling his civil rights.

The story is told in a most interesting way—through telephone conversations, letters, diaries, school memos, and discussions. You put the pieces together to follow a most unusual story.

This book is different from other books you might have read. At first the whole argument seems overblown. Then you will start to wonder—what is the truth in the end?

The Landry News by Andrew Clements
Simon & Schuster Books for Young Readers, 1999.

Cara Landry is assigned to Mr. Larson's fifth-grade class for reading, language arts, and social studies. Cara is a good student, but Mr. Larson is an awful teacher. Most parents in Carlton write to the principal to make sure their children are not placed in his class. Mr. Larson reads all the time, and his class is filled with heaps of newspapers and magazines, but the problem is this. Mr. Larson stopped teaching a long time ago. He ignores his classes and reads all day. This doesn't bother Cara at first because she sets up a little office in the class and begins writing a newspaper on her own.

Cara posts the newspaper titled "The Landry News" on the bulletin board. Mr. Landry is interested that all the class crowds around to read the paper. He goes to the back of the room to read himself. Then his jaw drops. Cara's paper declares that no teaching is going on in class.

When Mr. Larson tells his wife about Cara's paper, Mrs. Larson tells him that maybe the girl is looking for a teacher rather than being difficult. The teacher starts to face the truth. When, he thinks to himself, did he stop teaching? What can he do about it?

Cara's parents are caught in a bind. They've always encouraged Cara to tell the truth, but when does the truth need to be tempered with kindness? Cara thinks about her actions, and so does Mr. Larson.

As you read the book, you will find that people learn lessons all through their lives. Mr. Larson and Cara both undergo changes that will result in success in the end. To discover what happens, you'll want to read *The Landry News* by Andrew Clements.

The Library Card by Jerry Spinelli
Scholastic Press, 1997.

Jerry Spinelli won the Newbery Medal for his extraordinary book about a super hero kid called "Maniac McGee," and he still spins amazing stories such as the three tales in this book, *The Library Card.*

In the first story, "Mongoose," two friends named Weasel and Mongoose spend most of their time fooling around and getting in trouble. They are clever enough not to be caught vandalizing property by spray painting words and messages on buildings around town. You would never expect guys like this to enter a library. That's why you'll be intrigued when Mongoose pulls a plain blue card from his pocket, ends up in front of the public library, and goes into the building.

Mongoose doesn't know how the card works. He thinks it is a ticket to give to the lady inside. Instead, the lady tells him it isn't something to let you in. The card is something to let you take books out.

That is when Mongoose takes out a book titled *I Wonder,* and his world changes. Mongoose now enters the world where cicada bugs bury themselves underground for seventeen years and a special bird stays in the air for four years. Other birds ride on the backs on rhinos, and cockroaches can walk around for two weeks without heads. Books and libraries change Mongoose's life in ways you can only wonder about. Maybe they could change yours.

How would you react if your parents took away your TV rights for a whole week? In the second story of Jerry Spinelli's book, Brenda freaks. She watches all the soap operas, game shows, sitcoms, and commercials. She is the most compulsive television addict you will ever meet. Her parents' experiment to rid the house of TV shows turns Brenda into a subhuman being. She eats compulsively. She uses binoculars to watch the neighbors' TV. She puts rabbit ears antennas in her mouth.

Finally she ends up at the library, where she receives a letter from "The Books" to encourage her to read. As Brenda begins reading her own biography, she starts to remember what her life was like before she was addicted to television.

Are you addicted like Brenda? Is she cured? Could you return to books and find yourself whole and healthy again? You will be *driven* to find the answers in this far-fetched but fascinating story!

Two more stories appear in this book. One is called "Sonseray" about a homeless kid who finds peace and quiet in the library. The last story about April Mendez tells us about a girl who doesn't belong until she puts her library card in her pocket and rides a bookmobile every day. Read *The Library Card* to enjoy these unusual adventures!

Keen Jean Book Club: A Library Booktalk Program Series

The object of this program series is similar to the previous program planned for schools, but this is a more casual approach.

Materials Needed

Use the same list from the BNBR materials list with these differences.

1. Old blue jeans that participants bring from home (Have extra jeans available for those who forget.)

2. A portable sewing machine to sew the jeans shut (or a hot glue gun or heavy-duty needles and thread to sew by hand)

3. Several pairs of sharp scissors

4. Five feet of belting or cording for the two shoulder straps of each bag

5. Puffy paints, fabric markers in several colors, and other materials to decorate the bags

Procedure

1. In preparation, make a sample book bag and a jeans book vest to wear. Purchase a commercial jeans vest at a discount store and decorate it yourself with patches or use fabric markers and puffy paints to write titles of books all over the vest. If the vest has pockets, you can stuff them with pencils and index cards (see Fig. 8.1).

2. Wearing your vest, greet kids who have come to the first meeting of the Keen Jeans Book Club. Tell kids they will be making jeans bags today (have several on display). These bags will hold the books they read. At the end of the program you will tell them about some of the neat books they may check out.

3. Instruct kids to cut off the pant legs, using the sample on display as an example (see Fig. 8.2). Tell them to be careful not to cut off too much of the legs.

4. Participants then sew up the bottoms of the legs to form the base of the bag. Have adult volunteers on hand to help those kids who have never used a sewing machine.

5. Now sew on the straps. Each strap should be about thirty inches long. The straps might be tied tightly to belt loops on the jeans if you don't want to sew this part. The illustration in Figure 8.3 will give you an idea of what the keen jeans book bag should look like.

6. Let the children decorate their jeans bags if they wish.

7. Bring in a book cart with new books and titles from the list in this chapter's bibliography.

8. Do several booktalks as a demonstration.

9. Have the children check out the books they will share at the next session.

10. When the kids return another day, discuss the books in a casual "round-robin" fashion. Then guide the kids in becoming booktalkers, using the instructions of the BNBR program in the previous section. Pass out copies of the bookmarks on booktalking. Allow time for kids to work on booktalks.

11. Ask for volunteers to do booktalks. These are not "required," but tell kids the object of the book club is to be willing participants. Booktalking will be a part of every book club meeting.

12. Leave time for kids to check out more books.

13. In continuing sessions, intersperse the booktalks with other book activities found in the "Idea Springboards" section of this chapter.

14. The following sample booktalk program focuses on a theme that is a lot of fun to use in a public library setting.

Figure 8.1

Figure 8.2

Figure 8.3

Frogs and Toads: A Library Booktalk Program

In many fairy tales, frogs and toads have magical properties. Why is this? What if kissing a frog turned you into something else? What if you bought a toad, and it started talking? These books are all about such strange happenings.

Jennifer Murdley's Toad by Bruce Coville
Harcourt, Brace, Jovanovich, 1992.

The first book is one of the "Magic Shop" books written by Bruce Coville. Bruce lives in New York, where he shares his house with a cat. He has done many things besides writing books. One of his earlier occupations was making toys. When you read *Jennifer Murdley's Toad,* you may understand why Bruce is interested in magic shops and in the kind of adventures you will find in this book.

I won't tell you all about Jennifer, because you'll have to read to find out the whole story. I *will* tell you that Jennifer is a kid who really wants to be beautiful. She isn't, and even her friends tease her about that. It all started one day when her Dad had not done the laundry. He made Jennifer wear a clean pair of underpants that belonged to her brother. Yuck! Well, Jennifer made the mistake of telling her friends. After that, the teasing increased. In a state of desperation, Jennifer enters a magic shop, where she ends up buying a talking toad. Nothing is ordinary after that.

The talking toad gets Jennifer into trouble. Jennifer pretends to be studying to be a ventriloquist to protect the toad. The magic grows as the toad kisses Shanna, Jennifer's friend. Shanna turns into a toad. This toad business becomes a plague. Each person who changes into a toad is kissed by another person, who then turns into a toad. How will this end?

The Frog Princess of Pelham by Ellen Conford
Little, Brown, & Company, 1997.

Do you ever feel as if you would be better off if you were an orphan? Maybe you've had a fight with your Mom or Dad. Maybe you think life would be just fine if you were rich and lived with another relative. Think again. Chandler, the heroine of our story, is a rich orphan who lives with her only living relative, Horace. Horace wants to send Chandler off to camp for the summer. But Chandler is clever. She discovers a way to not go to camp and begin the perfect vacation.

Beware, Chandler! That cute guy Danny that you have a crush on is just about ready to do something that will change your life. He gives you what you've dreamed about. A kiss. The minute this happens, Chandler feels a weird feeling whoosh through her. When she opens her eyes, she sees a huge Reebok.

What happened? Why would a Reebok look huge to a girl? Well, a real girl wouldn't see it that way. You see, Chandler is no longer a girl. Somehow the kiss has changed her into a frog.

"I couldn't have done that!" said Danny. "You must have done it to yourself!"

Jennifer gives Danny a tongue lashing, but it is true. She has turned into a toad.

Throughout most of the book, Danny feels responsible for turning his classmate into a toad, so he does almost anything to help her. He protects Jennifer from dogs, finds froggy food for her to eat, and stands up to the army when they try to take the frog off to a laboratory to do experiments. How can a kid be so brave? How can Jennifer become a girl again? Will she change back in time?

Read Ellen Conford's humorous novel for yourself to discover the answers.

The Frog Princess by E. D. Baker
Bloomsbury Children's Books, 2002.

Even as a little girl, Princess Emeralda loved the swamp. She thinks it is more magical than a palace, but then, she isn't much of a princess. She laughs like a donkey. She is clumsy. And she definitely doesn't want to marry Prince Jorge. Unfortunately her mother is determined that the princess marry the prince. Life seems to be a pool of mud.

Then one day, Emma (the princess' nickname) meets Eadric. Eadric will become her best friend, but not at first. Eadric wants Emma to kiss him. Will she do it? Will Emma actually kiss him? After all, this is a frog! Will Emma turn Eadric into a prince who is nicer than Prince Jorge?

Let me tell you something shocking. Eadric does *not* change. Then what does happen? Remember, this is a fairy tale where magical happenings take place. Yes, Emma is the one who changes, and she turns into a frog herself. What will they do?

Will Emma's aunt, a beautiful witch, help them? Will another witch too ugly for words take pity on the frogs? Or will she lay a trap for them? Maybe the frogs can find their own solutions. Some of the story gets gross at this point. The frogs find concoctions I hate to mention. One is a jar labeled Lizard Lips. The frogs meet freaky animals along the way, a snake named Fang, a spider, and a bat. Should they trust them?

Without telling you the actual ending, let me remind you that this is a fairy tale, so the ending is magical. You may be surprised, but you won't be sorry if you check this story out for yourself. *The Frog Princess* by E. D. Baker.

Kids on Their Own: A Booktalk Program for Older Children

Kids, most of you probably know someone your age who does not live with both of his or her parents. Many children live with one parent, and some live with a guardian. Some kids feels isolated, as if they have to grow up in a tough world with little help to guide them. If you know someone like this, you'll identify with the books I've brought with me today. Bud, Nissa, and Angel are characters in books, but they aren't very different from kids you and I know.

Bud, Not Buddy by Christopher Paul Curtis
Delacorte, 1999.

If you could meet Christopher Paul Curtis, the author of this book, I know you would like him instantly. Christopher has a warm, friendly smile, a welcoming personality, and loves writing books for young people your age. He also may have beginner's luck. *The Watsons Go to Birmingham—1963*, his first book, was a Newbery Honor book. His second book, *Bud, Not Buddy,* won two big awards—The Coretta Scott King Award for the best book of the year written by an African American author, and the Newbery Award for the best children's book of the year. This is the first time any book has won both of these important honors.

Buddy, is a ten-year-old boy living during the Great Depression in the 1930s. Because Buddy's mother died when he was six and he doesn't know where his father lives, Buddy has been living in an orphanage. Then he is sent to live in a foster home, but he finds this unbearable. Buddy runs away. He doesn't know exactly where to go, but he knows he has to find the man mentioned on a flyer his mother had when she died. The flyer is about a jazz musician named Herman E. Calloway. Buddy somehow gets the idea that Calloway is his father. Maybe Buddy can find his way to Chicago to be reunited with his dad.

Check out *Bud Not Buddy* and trace Buddy's dangerous journey from Flint, Michigan, to Chicago, where he does meet Herman E. Calloway. Buddy is in for a disappointment. Herman E. Calloway isn't excited to see Buddy at all. In fact, he doesn't trust Buddy. How can Buddy prove he *is* Herman Calloway's son? Or is he Calloway's son? Will Buddy find a home after all? If you read the book to the end, you'll be surprised how the dramatic story ends. *Bud, Not Buddy* by Christopher Paul Curtis.

The Year of the Sawdust Man by A. LaFaye
Simon & Schuster, 1998.

Nissa Bergen in Alexandria LaFaye's book *The Year of the Sawdust Man* also lives during the 1930s. Unlike Buddy in the book you've just heard about, Nissa does not live in a northern city. She lives in a rural part of Louisiana, and she does have one parent. She used to have a close family, a warm circle of love and laughter. Nissa's mother entered into the world of fantasy and play, so she seemed more like a playmate than a mother. In fact, Mrs. Bergen even told Nissa that the little girl was "half adult" and, she, the mother, was "half child."

Even though Nissa understands that her mother is a free spirit who can't always be relied on, it is a terrible shock when Mama runs away. Nissa and her father cling to each other. Papa tries to comfort her as best he can. But she is in deep pain.

Nissa has so much to think about. Everyone in town gossips. They gossip about Mama. They ask Nissa rude questions. Why did Mama leave? Did she run off with another man? Nissa remembers her mother used to come back to the house with the smell of sawdust on her clothes. Did Mama go off with the black man who made furniture for the family? As the image of the "sawdust man" fills Nissa's mind, she tells herself that Mama might very well have run off with him.

After five months pass, Papa longs for a wife. As he becomes friends with Miss Lara Ross, a "proper" lady who wears gloves, Nissa has another worry. Is Papa planning to marry Miss Ross? Will Mama come back? Will Nissa ever hear from her mother again? You won't be able to put this book down once you get started. You'll want to know the answers to all these questions. You'll want to know more about Nissa and what happens to her mother. Read *The Year of the Sawdust Man* by A. Lafaye.

The Same Stuff as Stars by Katherine Paterson
Clarion Books, 2002.

If you have ever read *Great Gilly Hopkins* by Katherine Paterson, you know that her stories about kids on their own can be hard books to read. I don't mean the vocabulary is difficult—her stories grip you in the middle of your stomach, and that's what makes them hard to read in a painful way. Mrs. Paterson's latest book, *The Same Stuff as Stars,* will move you in the same way.

From the beginning of the book, we know that Angel Morgan is in trouble. Her father is in jail. Her mother drinks excessively. Angel has a feisty little brother, Bernie, who she has to look out for. Once in awhile, this sad little family goes to visit Daddy in jail. The prison guards are rude. No one really wants to go to the jail. How can life go on like this?

Things change. One day, Mama wakes Angel and Bernie and tells them to pack their suitcases for a trip. The kids have no idea where they are going, but they begin to get suspicious. Before long, Mama drives them to Great-Grandma's old wood shack. Inside, it's dark and stuffy and not very welcoming.

"I didn't really expect company," says the old woman huddled in blankets by the cold pot-bellied stove. There are no sheets on the beds, and only beans in a can to eat, but the children go to sleep that night at Grandma's. In the middle of the night, Angel wakes up. She sneaks around the house only to discover that her mother isn't there.

The next day, too, Mama isn't there. Has she left them? How will they get along with almost no food and a great-grandmother who needs help herself? What will keep Angel's spirit alive? That's when Angel meets a strange man with a telescope who teaches her about the stars. Every night Angel learns more about the stars and looks to the wonder of the sky. The beauty of these nights and her growing affection for Great-Grandmother makes all the difference in Angel's life.

This is not the end of the story. Other things happen. Some are scary. Some are surprising, and some are filled with a little hope. You'll have to read this book through completely to the end if you want to find out what happens to Angel and her brother. Read *The Same Stuff as Stars* by Katherine Paterson. You can't put it down once you start.

Other Booktalk Programs

This list could be endless, just as the topic of booktalks could fill many volumes, but here are a few names and random thoughts for you to create your own programs. The booktalk programs described in this chapter are planned around themes. Although this is one of my favorite ways to do booktalks, you can also do programs that include a variety of types of books. For example, in one session you might do booktalks on humorous books; at another time you could plan the program around biographies. You might do a miscellaneous booktalk program with favorite books written in the past two years, or a program on Newbery Honor books. You might do a program on a single author such as Katherine Paterson, who writes consistently excellent books set in different times and places. You could also do a program on a series of books such as the Time Warp Trio by Jon Scieszka.

The following list provides other themes, authors, and books for planning booktalk programs.

1. Books That Make You Think: *The Giver* by Lois Lowry (Houghton Mifflin, 1993), *The Last Book in the Universe* by Rodman Philbrick (Blue Sky Press, 2000), and *Tuck Everlasting* by Natalie Babbitt (Farrar, Straus and Giroux, 1975).

2. Books by Katherine Paterson. The choice is so vast, but a few of my favorites include *Great Gilly Hopkins, Bridge to Terabithia,* and a collection of short stories for Christmas, *Angels and Other Strangers.*

3. Books by E. L. Konigsburg. Varied topics and experiences. Try these. All are Newbery Medal or Honor books: *From the Mixed Up Files of Mrs. Basil E. Frankweiler* (Atheneum, 1967) , *The View from Saturday* (Atheneum, 1996), and *Jennifer, Hecate, MacBeth, William McKinley, and Me, Elizabeth* (Atheneum, 1967).

4. Fantasy Titles: *James and the Giant Peach* by Roald Dahl (Knopf, 1961), *Ella Enchanted* by Gail Carson Levine (HarperCollins, 1997), and *The Secret of Platform 13* by Eva Ibbotson (Dutton, 1998).

5. Miscellaneous Realistic: *Maniac McGee* by Jerry Spinelli (Little, Brown, 1990), *Joey Pigza Loses Control* by Jack Gantos (Farrar, Straus and Giroux, 2000), and *Itchy Richard* by Jamie Gilson (Clarion, 1991).

6. This and That: *Hatchet* by Gary Paulsen (Bradbury, 1987), *The Goats* by Brock Cole (Farrar, Straus and Giroux, 1984), and *One Eyed Cat* by Paula Fox (Bradbury, 1984).

7. Other Hard Times, Other Difficult Places: *I Never Saw Another Butterfly* edited by Hana Volavkova, *Number the Stars* by Lois Lowry (Houghton, 1989), *Out of the Dust* by Karen Hesse (Scholastic, 1997), and *Something Permanent* by Cynthia Rylant (Harcourt, 1994).

8. Dear Diary for Guys: *Dear Mr. Henshaw* by Beverly Cleary (William Morrow, 1983), *In Ned's Head* by Soren Olsson and Anders Jacobsson (Atheneum, 2001), and *Love That Dog* by Sharon Creech (Joanna Cotler Books/HarperCollins, 2001).

Idea Springboards: Activities to Develop

Name That Book: A Book and Picture Game

Test your ability to guess the titles of books from a picture clue. The Keen Jeans Book Club can make their own cards, or teen volunteers can make them to stump older elementary children from the book club.

Cut playing cards from card stock. On one side of the playing cards, provide the title and author of a book with a brief annotation. On the other side, supply a "picture clue" that you have drawn or find clip art from the Internet. Laminate cards so they will last for many sessions.

The leader simply holds up the picture side of the card to the group. The first person to identify the book receives a point. Another point is given for providing the author's name. Two points are given for telling what the book is about.

This game can be played in a small group, giving points to each player who successfully makes one of these identifications. The game can also be played in teams if you have many children participating.

You will certainly want to have copies of the books available so that kids can read the books mentioned in the game. To inspire your own thinking, my suggestions for books and picture icons follow.

1. A waffle: *Everything on a Waffle* by Polly Horvath. A girl becomes orphaned, goes to live with an uncle, and adjusts to her new life. She likes to cook different dishes, usually toppings for waffles. A recipe ends each chapter.

2. A hatchet: *Hatchet* by Gary Paulsen. A boy lost in the wilderness learns how to survive with only a hatchet.

3. A head sliced across the top: *In Ned's Head* by Soren Olsson and Anders Jacobsson. Ned keeps a diary, which he writes under a code name. He doesn't want anyone to read it because it's full of what's inside his head.

4. A wrinkled clock: *A Wrinkle in Time* by Madeleine L'Engle. Three children become involved in a time-warp fantasy where they meet unusual characters: some good and some evil.

5. A pizza with sun rays streaming from it: *A Pizza the Size of the Sun* by Jack Prelutsky. Humorously exaggerated poems cover a range of topics including a big pizza the size of the sun.

6. Flowers in a garden under moonlight with the number 12: *Tom's Midnight Garden* by Philippa Pearce. One night an old grandfather's clock strikes the number thirteen and the boy in this story meets a girl from a previous time period.

7. Two frogs, one with a crown: *The Frog Princess* by E. D. Baker. A princess kisses a frog only to be turned into a frog herself. Many fantastic adventures follow.

8. A large peach with a boy inside: *James and the Giant Peach* by Roald Dahl. Magic crystals spill on a peach tree causing it to grow big fruit. James crawls inside a peach to discover wonderful creatures and fantasy adventures.

Book Charades

Kids still like to join in a rousing game of charades. Instead of acting out songs, movies, and television shows, limit the categories to books. You know the rules. Divide the group into two teams. Each team writes down titles of books on index cards for the other team to guess. One by one each player draws a card prepared by the opposite team. The object of the game is to get your teammates to guess the book title using only actions and mimes, but no words. Proper names are not allowed. Hold up fingers for the number of words in the title. Chop one arm with the other hand to indicate syllables then hold up a finger to indicate which syllable is being acted out. Tug the ear for a "sounds like" word. And remember, no talking! Limit each player to three minutes. The team that guesses the most book titles wins. But provide prizes for everyone—cool pencils, bookmarks, or free used books from the library's book sale, for example.

Book Trivial Pursuit

Design your own game of trivia based on books in your library collection. Divide the group into teams. The team that answers the most questions correctly wins, but have prizes and refreshments for all.

Serve "book-related treats" such as pizza (related to Prelutsky's *A Pizza the Size of the Sun)* jelly beans (inspired by Harry Potter books), meatballs (inspired by *Cloudy with a Chance of Meatballs)* or chocolate brownies (inspired by *Charlie and the Chocolate Factory)*. The sample Book Trivia Cards will help you get started with your own brainstorming.

Question: What is the name of the main character in the book Dear Mr. Henshaw?

Answer: Leigh Botts

Question: What causes the peach to grow big in the book James and the Giant Peach?

Answer: Magic crystals

Question: What happened in Jennifer Murdley's Toad just before Jennifer goes into the magic shop?

Answer: Jennifer was cruelly teased by her classmates.

Question: Which book by Karen Cushman won the Newbery Award?

Answer: *The Midwife's Apprentice (Catherine Called Birdy* was an Honor book.)

Vested: A Power Suit for Book Lovers

Make your own book vest from a ready-made vest (discount stores or the Salvation Army are good sources) or cut out one from felt using the drawing in this chapter as an example (Fig. 8.1). Denim material or muslin can also be used if you are willing to do a little sewing or use a hot-glue gun to attach the basic vest pieces.

Add one or more pockets to hold notes or index cards that describe books.

This garment is great for teachers and librarians who are doing a booktalk program. Older kids can make their own during a workshop. Volunteers can make vests for reading incentive prizes or for members of the library book club.

Artistic people can embroider book characters. Everyone can photocopy book covers with color photocopies onto fabric and glue these on vests. Let your imagination and passion for books soar!

Book Discussion Groups

Book discussions in schools, libraries, church groups, household book club gatherings, and online chat groups are mushrooming in the twenty-first century. In my research I have found far more interest in this topic than I had dared to hope. Thousands of libraries, Web sites, and book stores provide suggestions for books to discuss. Articles and books on the topic give advice on how to run a successful group.

Basic considerations include the following:

Who: Who will be running the group, and who will be part of it? Is the teacher or librarian in charge, or will you choose an "outside expert." Is the group limited to a particular age or demographic? Parents and kids? Mothers and daughters?

What: What is your goal or goals? Why are you doing this? For entertainment? Education? Both? To promote reading or using the library? Will you have ground rules such as (e.g., speak clearly and loudly, do not interrupt).

Where: Where will you meet? Will it be the same location for every meeting?

When: What night will you meet? How often? How long will each session run?

How: How will you publicize the group? Invitations? Posters and flyers? Media (radio, television)? Direct contacts (kids who frequently visit the library)? How will the discussions begin and proceed? (Give author information, ask intriguing questions, serve book-related refreshments, ask adults to let kids talk first.) How will you choose and get the books? Will you charge for the books or provide library copies for everyone?

Book discussion groups, however you run them, provide wonderful opportunities for readers to share their favorite books and to connect with other readers. Parent-child groups let two generations discover more about what each thinks. Parents can get to know other children the same age as their children and therefore understand child development in general and in particular. Book discussions encourage verbal skills, communication, and can expand vocabularies. Leaders can urge participants to become more specific when they might otherwise simply say the book is "interesting," "enjoyable," or "fun." Insightful leaders will help participants create a nonjudgmental atmosphere in which everyone hears differing views. Stimulating leaders will seek positive comments about the book to begin and summarize the discussion at the end.

Suggested kinds of questions include the following:

1. Why do you think the author gave the book this particular title?

2. Which character is your favorite and why?

3. With which character do you not identify and why?

4. What main problem or situation needs to be resolved in the book?

5. Does this book remind you of others by the same author? Of other books on this theme?

6. What did you learn about yourself as you read this book?

7. What might you change about the book?

8. What is the theme or main idea in the book?

9. Are there details about the story, the setting, or characters that you particularly liked?

10. If the book could end in another way, what would you suggest?

11. What made the book worthwhile?

Book Journals

Why do some people seem to remember what they have read better than others? What can librarians and teachers do so they are better reader advisors? How can we improve our critical book evaluation skills?

These questions, I feel, are all related to the practice of keeping a book journal. Certainly reading and reading book reviews from different sources contributes to our individual critical evaluation skills. But thinking and writing out comments as we read also establishes the habit of reading with more deliberation and purpose.

Several of my best friends have kept their own book journals for years. Carol keeps her journal chronologically by the date she reads the books. She begins a new journal every year. Paula organizes her journal by topics or themes and limits her comments to a brief remark. I have done both, but tend to be more haphazard. I compile bibliographies periodically and encourage my staff to list titles by topics that library patrons ask for.

There is no one right or wrong way to keep a journal. Here are some ideas to consider:

1. Pretend that you are writing a diary or journal. Keep the "voice" of the journal as personal as your own style as if you are chatting to a friend about books.

2. Try to find a regular time to keep the journal, such as at lunch or just before bedtime.

3. Treat yourself to an attractive journal or cover a standard notebook with book postcards, book reviews, or clip art.

4. Leave a few pages at the back of the journal for titles that others recommend, with a note to jog your memory about why the book was recommended.

5. Tape book reviews from newspapers and journals into your own journal to help you choose what book to read next.

6. After several months of reading, make up your own "best books list." This will force you to evaluate and prioritize, just as book critics do.

7. Consider writing your comments in the form of a letter to a friend or the author of the book.

8. Break all the rules! Write whenever you like and vary the kind of remarks you make. Maybe you've finished or half-finished a book you genuinely don't like. You don't *have* to belabor a book you find worthless. Maybe the book inspires you to write a poem or a long review. Go ahead and follow your heart.

9. Write down new words and special sentences or thoughts that you want to remember.

10. Include sketches if you are artistic (or little doodles) along with your words.

9

Hooray for the USA

Celebrating our Heritage through Literature

How can a single chapter in a resource book cover the vastness of the United States, its history, government, the story of its diverse cultures, its honorable men and women, and the accomplishments of so many? How can a few thousand words due justice to this topic? Certainly, it cannot. I do hope, however, to spark an interest in exploring the United States through books and activities that you will use in classrooms, libraries, and communities with children.

The early years of the twenty-first century have thus far been dramatic and troubled times. Children in the past have lived through war, economic hardship, and upheaval. It is not a question of whether children now are living in more difficult times, but certainly they are living in an age of instant communications that seem to amplify distress.

Adults, especially educators, can and should provide young people with honest, high-quality materials for them to face the world in which we live. We need to know enough about child development to present age-appropriate materials and use them in thoughtful contexts.

As educators, we can be grateful that Eve Bunting has written honest, insightful accounts of topics such as the 1992 Los Angeles riots in *Smoky Night*. We are fortunate that Patricia Polacco, an excellent artist, can also tell such poignant stories as *Pink and Say* that evokes the emotional side of the Civil War. We can be glad that Dr. Robert Coles, the noted child psychiatrist, writer, and distinguished American, wrote *The Story of Ruby Bridges* about the remarkable African American girl who courageously entered an elementary school in New Orleans amid the angry crowds of prejudiced white people in 1960.

Historical accounts and textbooks, although vital for providing background information, cannot tell the stories in the way these books can. For every history lesson about the Civil War, I hope that classroom teachers will include a diary, fictional account based on the fact, or a poem to give children a more comprehensive view of that conflict. For every display of historical books or library program about crafts and cooking during the Civil War, I hope librarians will include a bibliography and book display with stories and poems that touch the heart.

If you are not familiar with Kieran Egan's outstanding book *Teaching as Story Telling: An Alternative Approach to Teaching and Curriculum in the Elementary School,* I heartily recommend that you read it. Egan makes a strong argument that using story is the most natural way to teach any subject because conflict or tension between opposing forces is intrinsic to all areas of knowledge. Egan demonstrates how you can look at the content you are required to teach and the curriculum goals and standards you must meet and then transform them into a story form that will capture the interest of your students more vividly than rote learning ever could.

The recent publishing trend of fictional historical diaries written by talented authors delights many librarians and teachers. I have noted with enthusiasm how popular these books are with both boys and girls. I have added dozens of titles from the "Dear America" and "My America" series to the children's collections in public libraries where I have worked. I find that kids are not only reading them, but asking for more. Kathryn Lasky's suffragette diary painfully opened my eyes about the living conditions of those early suffragettes who were held in American prisons.

Because this guide focuses on many topics with the intent of sharing stories, books, and literature-based activities, this chapter provides a sampler of books and activities in these areas. Rather than provide history lessons and a curriculum for social studies and government, I offer projects and activities to include in the classroom or library to enhance topics about the United States.

The children in your community may not have experienced a school bombing, but they witness them on television news. They frequently overhear adults discussing world terrorism. As I write this book, I see children in my own community affected by the 2003 war in Iraq. I grew into adulthood during the Vietnam War protests, and my children grew up as the Watergate hearings monopolized daytime TV. My young son worried about global issues so much that I sought the advice of a counselor, who wisely suggested I listen and not dismiss his insightful comments. "Reassure him that many caring adults are working on those very problems." Teachers and children's librarians face huge challenges working with today's youth. With your guidance, the children you teach or to whom you read will find thoughtful books to help them become caring, responsible future citizens in the country in which we live.

Books about the USA

Anderson, Joan. *The First Thanksgiving Feast*. Photographs by George Ancona. Clarion, 1984 (historical nonfiction).
    One of several historical documentary picture books by Anderson and Ancona, this text explores the events surrounding the Plymouth Colony story. Fictional dialogue between the pilgrims brings the history alive along with the photographs taken at the Plimouth Plantation in Massachusetts. Useful for reading aloud and creating interactive storytelling with elementary school children.

Anderson, Laurie Halse. *Fever 1793*. Simon & Schuster, 2000 (historical nonfiction).
    Matilda, a sixteen-year-old girl in Philadelphia, helps her mother run a coffeehouse as they face the growing horror of a yellow fever epidemic. Because Mattie's mother soon dies of the fever, most of the story tells of the young woman's plucky way to survive in the new nation. Well-drawn characters engage the reader in this tensely wrought tale. Older elementary students will eagerly learn about early American history from the book.

Cheney, Lynne. *America, a Patriotic Primer*. Illus. Robin Preiss Glasser. Simon & Schuster, 2002 (notable nonfiction).
    Lively ink and watercolor illustrations combine with Cheney's words. Each letter of the alphabet is used to describe such America-related terms as "C" for constitution, "D" for Declaration, and "S" for suffrage. (The author is the wife of Vice President Dick Cheney.)

Cobb, Mary. *A Sampler View of Colonial Life*. Millbrook Press, 1999 (projects).
    Describes colonial samplers and provides numerous exciting projects that kids can make, from cross-stitch to computer samplers.

Coles, Robert. *The Story of Ruby Bridge*s. Illus. George Ford. (biography) Scholastic, 1995.
    In 1960 Ruby Bridges, an African American child, was sent to a white school in New Orleans to desegregate the school. For months Ruby withstood angry mobs and empty classrooms, but she learned. After six months, she confronts the crowd by praying openly for the people. In time, several children returned to school, starting the pathway for desegregated schools in the United States.

The Declaration of Independence. Illus. Sam Fink. Scholastic, 2002 (historical nonfiction).

Fink's amusing illustrations with speech balloons amplify the meaning of Thomas Jefferson's text of our nation's founding document from 1776.

Fleming, Candace. *A Big Cheese for the White House.* DK Publishing, 1999 (historical nonfiction).

The citizens of Cheshire, Massachusetts, become angry when they discover President Jefferson is serving French cheese in the White House instead of their delicious American version. Elder John convinces the townsfolk to make an enormous cheese round and send it to the president to win him over. Kids love this little-known historical account.

Fritz, Jean. *Shh! We're Writing the Constitution.* Putnam's, 1987 (historical nonfiction).

Fritz's lively story of the summer of 1787 when fifty-five delegates met secretly to write the U.S. Constitution is filled with lively portraits of the personalities of our forefathers. Delegates argued about the length of the president's office, the idea of sovereign states, and the order of succession. Portions of the story can be turned into a script and acted out.

Giblin, James Cross. *The Amazing Life of Benjamin Franklin.* Scholastic, 2000 (biography).

In a "long picture book," the well-known nonfiction author Giblin tells a lively narrative of Franklin's eventful life. The young reader learns about Franklin's early career in journalism, his community service, his interest in science, and, most significantly, the many accomplishments that distinguished him as a statesman during the colonial period and early days of a new nation.

Keller, Laurie. *The Scrambled States of America.* Henry Holt, 1998 (notable nonfiction).

Stuck in the middle of the country, Kansas decides to have a states party so everyone can get to know each other. Missouri and Iowa plan the party, and all the states have so much fun that they trade places. Excited at first, the states soon begin to complain. Florida is freezing in Minnesota's place, Arizona doesn't like South Carolina's ocean waves because it ruins her hair, and Kansas feels homesick at sea because he changed places with Hawaii. Sidebar conversations and hilarious illustrations add to the fun and will inspire numerous class projects.

King, David C. *Civil War Days.* John Wiley & Sons, 1999 (projects).

Part of the "American Kids in History" series, this book provides commentary on Civil War life and introduces "hands-on" projects including recipes, games, and crafts. Also in this series: *Pioneer Days* (1997).

Kroll, Steven. *Ellis Island, Doorway to Freedom.* Holiday House, 1995 (historical nonfiction).

Brief history of the famous island in New York Harbor that became an immigration station for the United States is illustrated with soft pencil drawings and watercolor.

Leedy, Loreen. *Celebrate the 50 States.* Holiday House, 1999 (notable nonfiction).

Each state is represented with a picture and sidebar that includes basic facts and commentary. The appendix includes answers to questions that appear throughout the text and a big map of the country.

McCully, Emily Arnold. *The Ballot Box Battle.* Knopf, 1996 (historical nonfiction).

Based on historical notes about Elizabeth Cady Stanton's life, the author tells her own story about a little girl, Cordelia, who meets the distinguished leader of women's suffrage in 1880. Cordelia accompanies Stanton to the voting booth, and despite the fact men deny Stanton the vote, she vows to continue the fight. Cordelia resolves to continue the battle for women's rights.

McPherson, James M. *Fields of Fury, the American Civil War*. Atheneum, 2002 (historical nonfiction).

The Pulitzer Prize–winning author of other Civil War books, McPherson has written this outstanding narrative of American's deadliest war. Maps, numerous photographs of the day, and soldiers' anecdotes make this an outstanding source for young people.

Myers, Walter Dean. *Patrol, An American Soldier in Vietnam*. HarperCollins, 2002 (historical nonfiction).

This story-poem of a young African America soldier meeting the enemy and fighting face-to-face, will help children today understand this difficult period in American history. Based on Myers own experience in Vietnam, the emotions and grim reality of the story are further enhanced by Anne Grifalconi's stirring collage illustrations.

Osborne, Mary Pope. *My Secret War: The World War II Diary of Madeline Beck*. Scholastic, 2000 (historical nonfiction).

Part of the popular *Dear America* series, this fictional diary tells the story of a Long Island girl who keeps a diary between 1941 and 1942 while her father is in the navy during World War II. In an epilogue, the author provides historical background and photographs of the times including a recipe for War Cake that uses little sugar, no eggs, and no milk because these ingredients were rationed.

Panzer, Nora, ed. *Celebrate America in Poetry and Art*. Hyperion Books, 1994 (notable nonfiction).

Stunning works of art from a painting of Maine's coastland by Winslow Homer to folk-art works by Jacob Lawrence and Maria Alquilar accompany a wide range of poems by notable poets such as Carl Sandburg and James Weldon Johnson.

Perl, Lila. *It Happened in America: True Stories from the Fifty States*. Henry Holt, 1992 (notable nonfiction).

The author has included a true story for each state with questions and answers about its history. The stories can be read or told to students and are treasures for those who value the "story" behind history.

Quasha, Jennifer. *Jamestown: Hands on Projects about One of America's First Communities*. Rosen, 2001 (projects).

After a brief introduction to Jamestown, the first permanent English settlement in America, this well-illustrated book provides step-by-step instructions to making a variety of kid-pleasing projects. Included are land maps, model houses, and beeswax candles.

Rockwell, Anne. *Only Passing Through: The Story of Sojourner Truth*. Knopf, 2000 (biography).

Picture book text with evocative paintings by R. Gregory Christie tell the story of this famous African American woman, born into slavery, who becomes one of the most important spokespersons for freedom in American history. Taking the name Sojourner Truth, she travels across the country delivering her messages and songs of slavery as an inspiration to all people who seek freedom and justice.

Rockwell, Ann. *They Called her Molly Pitcher*, Knopf, 2002 (biography).

Wife of William Hays, a barber who joined Washington's colonial army at Valley Forge, Molly went along to cook and tend to the sick. Eventually Molly proves her mettle by bringing water to the thirsty soldiers and fires a cannon when her husband is injured on the battlefield. History remembers her as "Molly Pitcher," but the brave young woman preferred the title Washington conferred on her during the Revolutionary War, "Sergeant Molly."

St. George, Judith. *So You Want to Be President*? Illus. David Small. Philomel, 2000 (notable nonfiction).

St. George's amusing text reveals little-known facts and observations about the presidents. For example, the reader learns Taft had a great sense of humor, McKinley didn't like to dress up, and Harding admitted he was not fit for office. Small's droll illustrations won him the Caldecott Medal for this book.

Vaughn, Marcia. *The Secret to Freedom*. Lee and Low, 2001 (historical nonfiction).

Great Aunt Lucy tells her niece the story of her life when she was a slave in South Carolina. Lucy and her brother Albert found out about a secret code among the slaves, which used quilt patterns to direct people to freedom. Albert uses the code when he escapes to the North.

Programs and Activities

Starring the USA: A Public Library Program

Plan this program ahead with elementary school children. Children from a book club or those interested in doing creative dramatics can practice the script, adding their own lines as appropriate. Ask families to bring regional food favorites along with a recipe, or have Library Friends groups and volunteers cook dishes suggested in this section. This will be an evening of food and educational play.

Materials Needed

1. Scripts with student writing added (see model that follows)

2. American flags; U.S. maps; red, white, and blue balloons for decorations

3. A table for food decorated with red, white, and blue crepe paper and signs for each dish; supply copies of the recipes for each dish.

4. Paper plates, napkins, plastic tableware

5. Printed menus for the State Dinner (optional)

6. A costume for Uncle Sam or Miss Liberty, created, rented, or borrowed (Uncle Sam's costume might be as simple as a patriotic paper top hat in stars and stripes; Miss Liberty's might consist of a silver paper crown, a ribbon banner worn across the chest, and a silver cardboard torch or candle.)

7. Posterboard and sticks to make a sign for each state in the union (The sign might be shaped like the state for extra fun.)

Procedure

1. Before you start this program, provide script outlines to children, and hold a playwriting workshop for kids to complete the state speeches. Not all states have to have speeches, especially if just a few children come to this session.

2. Use the script provided in this section. Because all fifty states join in the roll call of states, children may double up roles. For example, the group of kids might all choose a state from a particular region. For example, six states make up New England. After the Uncle Sam calls that region, six more kids or the same six kids can become the Mid-Atlantic states. The South has twelve states. If you don't have that many children, let some kids take the role of two states.

3. At the end of this writing and practicing session, you should be ready for the actual program, to which parents and other kids will be invited.

4. On the night of the program, decorate the library with the materials listed earlier.

5. Dressed as Uncle Sam or Miss Liberty, you welcome the crowd and invite them to place their food on the State Dinner table. During the first part of the program, participants enjoy a State Dinner. Explain to the crowd that a State Dinner on the national level usually refers to a White

House dinner that hosts important dignitaries. The library's State Dinner is in honor of the community, and those present are the dignitaries.

6.   Feature dishes from several states, or focus on foods from your own state or region. Have children and parents bring their favorite dish with copies of the recipe. The following menu will serve as a starter list for your inspiration.

Menu for State Dinner

Choose dishes of your own region, adding recipes of your own. The library can serve a cold and a hot beverage and provide dinnerware, described in the materials list.

New England States
> Maine blueberry pancakes
> Massachusetts cranberry muffins
> Vermont easy maple syrup for ice cream or pancakes

Middle Atlantic States
> Maryland crab dip
> Pennsylvania funnel cakes

Southern States
> Georgia peach crumble
> Mississippi chocolate mud pie

The Midwestern States
> Iowa baked pork chops
> Missouri Ozark pudding
> Wisconsin cheese soup

The Mountain States
> Colorado chili cheese puff
> Idaho potato casserole

The Southwestern States
> New Mexico Indian fry bread
> Texas barbequed brisket

The Pacific States
> Alaska salmon spread with crackers
> California strawberry soup or fruit bowl
> Hawaiian coconut-banana breakfast cup

7.   Provide copies of the recipes that children bring to share with others. Display children's cookbooks, as well as those in the library's collection. Decorate the tables with red, white, and blue paper tablecloths and add symbols from the states such as cactus plants for Arizona, bowls of peaches for Georgia, oranges for Florida, a pineapple for Hawaii, potatoes for Idaho, small log cabins for Illinois, corn for Iowa, sunflowers for Kansas, storyteller dolls or chili peppers for New Mexico, cowboy hats for Texas, maple sugar candy or a bottle of maple syrup for Vermont, cheese wedge or slices for Wisconsin, and so on.

8.   Serve food buffet style, and then gather the players and audience for the performance.

9.   Perform the play "Let's Play We Are the USA" script that follows.

Let's Play We Are the USA

Uncle Sam or Miss Liberty begins the show. Each state says its name and holds up its sign when called on. After the roll call of each region, Sam or Liberty ask the states in that region to tell more about themselves. Not all states need do this, but the states in your region may all want to provide details. The specific script at the end gives students ideas for possible speeches.

S = Uncle Sam
L = Miss Liberty

S or L: Welcome, people of the United States. Our USA Players will now treat you to a little drama that celebrates all the states of this great country.
(Turns to players who are standing in groups to the right and left of S or L.)
Welcome States of the USA. I think you're great in countless ways. First, I'll call off the roll to see if everyone is here. New England states, count off by shouting your name after I call you!
Connecticut? (*Note: each state answers as its name is called*), Maine, Massachusetts, New Hampshire, Rhode Island, and Vermont!
Now tell us more if you'd like to do. Oh, tell us your capital, will you?
Now, the Mid-Atlantic states, it's your turn.
Remember just like before.
Shout your name when I call on you!
Delaware, Maryland, New Jersey, New York, Pennsylvania, and Washington, D.C.!

NY: I don't think Washington, D.C., is a state! I protest!

S or L: Let's all be friendly. I won't argue your point. I shall repeat. Shout out your name when I call on your state. (*Repeats names of the Mid-Atlantic states. Continue as before.*) Thank you, Mid-Atlantic.
We're moving down South where the days are warm.
Southern states, it's now your turn.
Alabama, Arkansas, Florida, Georgia, Kentucky, Louisiana, Mississippi, North Carolina, South Carolina, Tennessee, Virginia, and let's not forget you, West Virginia. (*Continue as before.*)

S or L: States of the Midwest. It's your turn.
Call out your name so we can learn.
Illinois, Indiana, Iowa, Michigan, Minnesota, Ohio, and last, Wisconsin. (*Proceed as before*)
Mountain States, stand up proud!
Speak your names before this crowd!
Colorado, Idaho, Montana, Utah, last comes Wy-o-ming!
Sing, sing, sing! (*Proceed as before*)
Southwest beauties, tell us your names
You all know how to play this game.
Arizona, Nevada, New Mexico, Oklahoma, and last but not least, big old Texas! (*Continue as before.*)
At last, we've come to the edge of the country. Hanging out there are states of the great Pacific.

Alaska, California, Hawaii, Oregon, and up in the corner, rainy Washington.
(Note: Sample scripts for a few states composed in rhyme could serve as models, although the states do not have to rhyme their speeches.)

Maine: Maine with a capital in Augusta
Taste our lobsters and our fish
Blueberry pie makes quite a dish
Sail around our rocky shores
Watch our seagulls fly and soar
We are called the Pine Tree State
We all think that Maine is great!

Colorado: Colorado, prettiest of them all
Denver, our capital is one mile tall
Come to a rodeo, visit our zoos
See the mountains whatever you do
Bring your camera to our state
Colorado is simply great!

California: California sun never stops
Sacramento our capital, one of the top
Cities to visit like big L.A.
San Francisco, see its bay
Hollywood and Disneyland
Clap your hands|
What a state
We all know California's great!

The Story of American History:
A School Program for Writing and Story Sharing

American history is not the recitation of dates. American history is the telling of our nation's story. Encourage children to create their own stories based on historical events they have researched. These can be written or told. Incorporate the ideas below for this program in your school for a program that is conducted over several sessions.

Materials Needed

1. Small notepaper for "comfort notes"

2. Diaries, notepads, or small notebooks for the Historical Diary

3. Scripts and costumes created from clothes found at home

4. Material for banners, as indicated in Springboard section

Procedure

Session I

1. Introduce the Step into History Activity described in this section. (This can be done by the librarian, media specialist, or in a school setting by the history teacher.) The sample script I have provided is one I wrote many years ago to share with school children at Thanksgiving time.

2. After reading the creative dramatics script, have children pick a character from history to research. Show children how to find biographical material and books about American History in the library and on the Internet, so they can create their own scripts for historical figures.

3. At the following session, children share their findings and their written stories aloud with the class.

Session II

1. Ask children to share their historical findings and stories with the group.

2. Explain to children that many women and children wrote comfort notes to soldiers during the Civil War. Ask them to write their own notes of comfort. This activity also relates to recent times during which many American children have written to family members or friends fighting in the Middle East. Use this writing exercise as an opportunity for children to learn about the Civil War.

3. Remind children that even after the slaves were freed, they did not have the same rights as white people. Obtaining civil rights was an issue from the moment the war ended, but it reached a critical level with the beginning of the civil rights movement in the 1950s. Select a number of history books and biographies focusing on the theme of civil rights for children to check out. Be certain to include books about Martin Luther King Jr., Rosa Parks, Ruby Bridges, and other civil rights activists.

4. Give the children small notepads or diaries to compose a journal as if they are living in the 1960s during the civil rights movement. Encourage children to interview or discuss this time period with a relative or a neighbor.

5. Have children make memorial banners using the instructions in the Springboard section. Hang these banners around the room. Shapes and designs for these banners appear in Figure 9.1. Text for typical banners also appears at the end of this chapter. Leave the banners hanging for the next session

Session III

1. At the final meeting, have children read from their diaries, using the banners as backdrops.

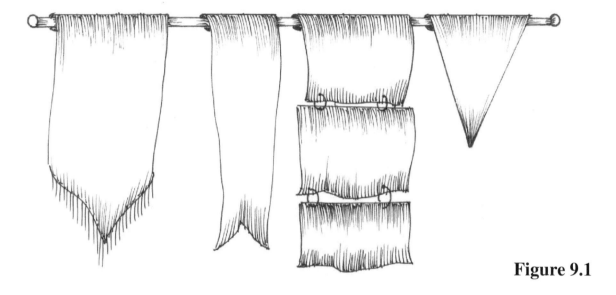

Figure 9.1

Step into History: A Creative Dramatics Script

The Big Feast by Susanna Winslow
Set in Plymouth, Massachusetts, 1621
Inspired by *The First Thanksgiving Feast* by Joan Anderson

My name is Susanna Winslow, wife of Edward Winslow, and I'm a saint.

Oh, perhaps I should explain. There are many of us who boarded the ship *Mayflower* in September of this past year, 1620. Aye—you must be children from another time. My talk must sound strange to you. But I am not a stranger. I am a saint.

You see, those of us who came to this new land to worship in our own way did not want to belong to the Church of England. We separated from the old church, so we are called separatists. We call ourselves "saints." The other people who came with us we call "strangers." Oh there are many good strangers. One of the strangers you might have heard of is Miles Standish. He's a good man, but he is not one of us.

I would like to tell you about our long trip last year. Aye, and what a trip. We left on our ship and sailed and sailed. For sixty-six days we sailed over rough seas. It was terrible. Cold, no room, little food. But we landed at last in the place we call Plymouth.

That first winter was dreadful cold. Winter set in. Over one-half of us died. If it weren't for the red-skin people who brought us fish and showed us how to plant, none of us might be here today.

I will never forget when the Indian named Samoset came to us. He spoke English. I praised the Lord. Samoset said to us "Welcome, Englishmen." Later he brought a friend named Squanto, who taught us how to grow corn. Later he brought Massasoit, chief of the great Wampanoag nation to sign a peace agreement.

Our Governor William Bradford brought us together. I'm proud to say my husband Edward is one of his able assistants. Several of us remembered that back in England at this time of year we have a harvest festival. My husband asked Governor Bradford if it might be a good idea to have a festival here. The Governor said we should have prayers and a day of thanks for our new land. My husband said he favored a feast too. Well, Governor Bradford agreed we could do both.

Now we are preparing for our big feast. We have so much to be grateful for. We have cod and ham. Berries grow in the woods around us. And we have corn.

We've invited our Indian friends to come. We'll have a happy feast. May all of you enjoy your own feast of Thanksgiving in your own homes, children. Farewell, and blessings to all of you.

Idea Springboards: Activities to Develop

Time Line Alive

Select important dates from a period of American history. Write a date and event on a sign. Select about ten dates, one for each year in a particular decade.

Students can consult time line books to make their own signs. For the decade of the 1950s, I came up with these dates and events:

1950 North Korean soldiers invade South Korea in June, and the Korean War begins

1951 Ethel and Julius Rosenberg were tried and found guilty for passing on American military secrets to Russian agents.

1952 King George VI of England dies

1953 Elizabeth, daughter of the late King George, is crowned queen of England

1954 U.S. Supreme Court rules that segregation in schools is a violation of the Fourteenth Amendment to the Constitution

1955 The U.S. Air Force Academy opens in Colorado

1956 Dwight Eisenhower is reelected president of the United States

1957 Queen Elizabeth visits the United States and addresses the United Nations

1958 President Eisenhower says the United States will stop all nuclear testing with the understanding that the Soviet Union will also do so. The agreement lasts until 1961.

1959 Castro is sworn in as prime minister of Cuba

To make the time line come alive, arrange chairs in a long line. Place a sign on each chair. Play a John Phillip Sousa march and tell children to march around the chairs. When the music stops, all children take seats. Starting with the earliest date, each student in order reads a year and event from the sign. This is an excellent way for children to understand kinesthetically the concept of a time line.

Continue this approach by having children go to computer catalogs or library shelves to find a book published the same year as the date they read aloud in the previous activity. You could simplify this exercise by having a book cart full of children's picture and chapter books published in the 1950s. This educational activity is like a game for children and should make history lively for them.

Who's Who in Women's American History: A Guessing Game

Play this game like Trivial Pursuit. Give a description of each famous American woman, then ask teams of children to guess the person. You will need to make a long list. The following examples will help you begin.

Examples of famous American women and their accomplishments

1. Known for her speech "Ain't I a Woman?" (Sojourner Truth)

2. Famous aviator whose plane was lost over the Pacific Ocean in 1937 (Amelia Earhart)

3. Well known Revolutionary War heroine who was given the title "Sergeant" by George Washington (Molly Pitcher)

4. First American woman to earn a medical degree (Elizabeth Blackwell)

5. Wrote *Uncle Tom's Cabin,* the book Lincoln said started the Civil War (Harriet Beecher Stowe)

6. Wrote *Little Women* and was the daughter of a famous American educator (Louisa May Alcott)

7. Made nineteen trips on the Underground Railroad to free numerous slaves (Harriet Tubman)

8. Founded the American Red Cross (Clara Barton)

9. African American woman who refused to give up her seat on a bus in Montgomery, Alabama, starting the bus boycott in 1955, a significant event in Civil Rights history (Rosa Parks)

10. Led a women's rights convention in Seneca Falls, New York, in 1848 (Elizabeth Cady Stanton)

Memorial Banners for American Heroes

Have each student select an American leader or hero to add to the memorial wall in your classroom or library. You or the children can make the banners of fabric, heavy paper, or brightly colored posterboard, featuring the name of the hero printed neatly across the top. If fabric is used, the banners can be hung from a long pole.

See the illustration in Figure 9.1 for an example of how to hang banners. The banners could have a drawing or a fact about the hero, or simply write the name with birth and death dates below it.

10

Heart to Heart and Hand to Hand

Courage, Power, and Healing through Children's Books

A child's world is not a place of innocence, as artist-author Maurice Sendak has shown us through his profound picture books, beginning with *Where the Wild Things Are*. If we ever doubted or denied this fact, the events of September 11, 2001, made it impossible to do so any longer.

Many adults try to protect children from fairy-tale witches or realistic stories found in newspapers. Others freely allow young children to watch television news with crime reports and scenes of bloody battles—and no discussion follows. Children are left alone to sort out what they have seen. These children watch endless cartoons with fighting and fierce warriors. Many of us worry that some children left unattended in front of the television might well turn to violence themselves when confronted with difficult situations in their lives.

Other adults choose to surround children with love and courage amid the world of books, with such titles as *Smoky Night* by Eve Bunting, or to provide wings through literature and let the spirit soar as Christopher Myers does in *Wings*. These are complex times in which to guide children, but the books listed in this chapter and their accompanying activities may provide you new sources with which to work.

During the past twenty-five years, children's books—not only longer fiction and nonfiction, but picture books as well—have opened our eyes to experience the horrors of atomic war and violence through titles about topics such as Hiroshima and the Oklahoma City bombings. Historical picture books such as *Pink and Say* or *Yellow Star* remind us of hard lessons learned in the past that can keep us aware of injustice as we continually struggle in a world of intolerance.

Concerned parents, teachers, and librarians work to counteract violence and conflict in positive ways. Most educators agree that building self-esteem is the first step. Preschool and primary-age children can understand Nancy Carlson's simple message, "I like you, and I like me," from her book *I Like Me!* Character education books and programs build on this base in developing character traits such as accepting others, valuing cooperation over competition, taking responsibility, and sharing our gifts.

The scope of this chapter is both broad and highly selective. It does not include religious books, but it does examine books of the spirit. It touches on historical records, stories of inspiration, and short poetic texts that praise the earth and people of courage. Picture books about animals and people who inspire, picture books in children's own words about peace, and picture books of joyful diversity have been selected.

Special effort has been made to bypass didactic books, sentimental words that tend to sugarcoat obvious pain and struggle, and books that do not allow children to ask intelligent questions and give them reassuring, thoughtful responses. We as adults do not always have answers, but we can provide reasonably hopeful messages. Children, of course, cannot take on the adult world, but they can be given wise, age-appropriate books of courage, power, and healing. May the choices in this chapter guide you as you work with the children in your care.

Books about Courage, Power, and Healing

Alexander, Lloyd. *The King's Fountain*. Illus. Ezra Jack Keats. Dutton, 1971, 1989.
    A king decides to build a great fountain below his palace that will cut off the city's water supply to its citizens. A poor man tries to find someone wise enough, brave enough, and well spoken enough to convince the king to rethink his plan. No one agrees, so the man goes to the palace himself. At first the king is irate, but he finally listens to the simple man's wise words and changes his mind.

Angelou, Maya. *Life Doesn't Frighten Me*. Illus. Jean-Michel Basquiat. Stewart, Tabori & Chang, 1993.
    Angelou's strong text in poetic form encourages children to acknowledge their fears but move ahead with courage. Basquiat's angry, childlike paintings complement the text and add a passionate note to the poem.

Bang, Molly. *The Paper Crane*. Greenwillow, 1985.
    Based on an ancient Japanese folktale, this story tells of an old man whose restaurant has little business until one day a stranger comes to eat. Instead of paying for his meal with money, the man makes an origami crane, gives it to the restaurant owner, and tells him a dancing bird will appear whenever he claps his hands. This happens, and many people come to the restaurant to eat and see the wonderful crane. One day, the stranger finally returns and plays his flute to make the crane appear. Together they fly off, never to be seen again. In the end, people continue to come to the "Paper Crane" restaurant to eat and hear the story again and again.

Berkley, Laura. *The Keeper of Wisdom*. Barefoot Books, 2000.
    In this story told in legend style, an old beggar woman peddles her books in a magnificent city. The mayor laughs at her for trying to sell the books of wisdom, but when the city is in need, he realizes his folly and buys the last books she has.

Bruchac, Joseph. *Between Earth and Sky: Legends of Native American Sacred Places*. Harcourt Brace, 1996.
    This collection, a series of short tales and poems in the Native American tradition along with Thomas Locker's glowing illustrations introduce readers to sacred places. Cheyenne, Hopi, and Wampanoag legends, together with scenes of mountains and deserts, will inspire meditation and poetry writing.

Bunting, Eve. *Riding the Tiger*. Clarion, 2001.
    A tiger convinces ten-year-old Danny to get on its back. Ignoring his inner voice, the boy accepts the risk, but soon learns that getting on the tiger is far easier than trying to get off. The story serves as a metaphor for making unwise choices and has excellent potential for discussions with older children.

Bunting, Eve. *Sunshine Home*. Illus. Diane de Groat. Clarion, 1994.

Eve Bunting's numerous books poignantly tell children about delicate and troublesome issues and concerns in our world. They are honest and careful in the treatment of topics such as visiting a grandmother in the nursing home, which is the focus of this book. The adults pretend there is nothing wrong with the grandma, who is being treated for a broken hip, but Timmie is perceptive enough to realize his family members are covering up their distress. He bravely addresses the emotional side of the problem, thus helping everyone realize how much they love one another.

Carle, Eric. *Draw Me a Star*. Putnam, 1992.

The artist in the story draws his own star and a world of living creatures and heavenly bodies. The moon beckons him to draw a star, and the star beckons him to hold on to it. This magical text and vivid illustrations inspire readers and listeners to explore their own creativity.

Coerr, Eleanor. *Sadako*. Illus. Ed Young. Putnam, 1993.

Coerr's picture book version of her longer story tells about a young Japanese girl who develops leukemia because she was exposed to the radiation of the atom bomb dropped on Hiroshima in 1945. An old legend that says that by folding one thousand origami cranes, the sick can become well. Sadako attempts to do this, but she dies before she can complete the task. Friends finish the cranes so that she will be buried with all one thousand of them. Today a statue of Sadako stands in Hiroshima Peace Park to remind people of the girl, her courage, and the tragedy of war.

Cordova, Amy. *Abuelita's Heart*. Simon & Schuster, 1997.

A young girl and her grandmother walk around the beautiful landscape in the Southwest and share feelings and the significance of these places as part of their heritage. A recipe for the "Happiness Meal" appears at the end of the book.

Cutler, Jane. *The Cello of Mr. O*. Illus. Greg Couch. Dutton, 1999.

A concert cellist plays in the neighborhood square in an unnamed war-torn city. One day, when the man is resting against a nearby building, a mortar shell destroys his cello. A little girl slips a drawing of the old man under his door to encourage him. Finally, he finds the courage to return to the square to play a harmonica, the tunes of which may be small compared to those of the cello, but they make the people who listen feel less afraid.

Goodman, Robin F., and Andrea Henderson Fahnestock. *The Day Our World Changed: Children's Art of 9/11*. Introduction by Rudolph W. Giuliani. Abrams, 2002.

Commentary and essays by prominent New Yorkers accompany stunning drawings and paintings by children after the terrorists' attacks on the World Trade Center. Among the brilliant words are an ink and watercolor painting titled *They Saw, They Conquered, We Cried*, an untitled torn-paper collage of a plane tearing into the first tower, and a stark depiction of the towers in black and white titled "Memorial" that also appears on the cover. This project was the unique collaboration of New York University's Child Study Center and the Museum of the City of New York.

Gray, Libba Moore. *My Mama Had a Dancing Heart*. Orchard, 1995.

A young woman who has become a ballet dancer lovingly recalls her mama who had a "dancing heart" and the many ways they shared dancing throughout their years together.

Hamanaka, Shelia. *Peace Crane*. Morrow Junior, 1995.

In this poetic text with stunning oil paintings, the author tells of the bombing of Hiroshima and the legend of the peace cranes associated with Sadako.

Hucko, Bruce. *A Rainbow at Night: The World in Words and Pictures by Navajo Children*. Chronicle Books, 1997.

Beautiful drawings by children are accompanied by quotes and an explanation of Navajo beliefs. Sidebars provide educational activities to use with children.

Levitas, Mitchel, ed. *A Nation Challenged: A Visual History of 9/11 and Its Aftermath*. The New York Times/Scholastic, 2002.

Outstanding color photographs and brief text take the reader back to the never-to-be-forgotten morning when planes commandeered by terrorists struck the World Trade Center and Pentagon, and another plane that may have been heading for the White House crashed in a Pennsylvania field. Told chronologically, the book focuses on that fateful day in September of 2001, and then traces the aftermath.

My Wish for Tomorrow. Tamborine Books/William Morrow, 1995

This unusual book was produced by a collaboration of Jim Henson Publishing and the United Nations and features a foreword by Nelson Mandela. The words and pictures are by children from all over the world, expressing their wishes for peace and prosperity for all people. The book is timeless, speaking to all ages and for all times.

Myers, Christopher. *Wings*. Scholastic, 2000.

Ikarus Johnson, a black child in a large city, wears wings to school. Classmates taunt him, but Ikarus uses his wings to gain his own sense of identity.

Polacco, Patricia. *Pink and Say*. Philomel, 1994.

In this deeply felt story set in the Civil War, Say Curtis, a young Union soldier from Ohio, meets Pinkus Aylee, a black soldier. The two escape from Confederate soldiers and find their way to Pink's home, where they are fed and cared for until the Confederates catch up with them. Say survives the war but calls out for all generations, including present-day readers, to remember Pink, who would not live to see a better time.

Rubin, Susan Goldman. *Fireflies in the Dark; The Story of Friedl Dicker-Brandeis and the Children of Terezin*. Holiday House, 2000.

Friedl was sent to Terezin, the "model" Nazi camp, to teach art to children held there briefly before being sent to one of the death camps. Through this remarkable young woman, children were given a respite from their fears and encouraged to express themselves through the arts. Friedl did not survive, nor did the majority of children sent to this camp. Goldman's touching story illustrated with the children's art is a testament to courage in the midst of perhaps the most horrifying period in history.

Programs and Activities

Follow Your Star: A Special Public Library Program about Life's Gifts

The inspiration for this activity comes from the books in this chapter's bibliography and a program I attended at the America Library Association's 2002 Annual Conference in Atlanta. The program activity is described later in the "Beaded Blessings Project." It is designed for children nine years and older.

Materials Needed

1. Colored paper, markers, paints and pastels, or crayons

2. Rayon, silk, rough-textured cotton, and tapestry remnants cut into four- to eight-inch squares or circles (Have enough squares or circles for each child to have two pieces.)

3. Long-eye needles, several packages

4.   Several spools of strong thread

5.   About twelve dozen beads with holes large enough for needles to go through them

6.   Six to eight yards of narrow ribbon in different colors to go with the fabric

7.   Small squares of paper, about three-inch square

8.   Pencils and pens

9.   A pair of safe scissors for every child

10.   A copy of Eric Carle's *Draw the Star* and another book from the list in step six of the procedures

Procedure

You may wish to prepare in advance by assembling a sample pouch to show the children before they begin.

1.   Announce the name of the program, then ask children to tell the group what the phrase "Follow Your Star" means to them. Who are their stars?

2.   Read Eric Carle's *Draw Me a Star*. Discuss the book briefly in terms of what a star looks like and ask children to draw a sketch of a star. Notice that there is no single way to draw a star. Carle's instructions create an eight-point star that looks something like a double star. The end pages of the book are filled with asymmetrical five-point stars.

3.   Provide children with paper, paints, markers, pastels, or crayons to decorate and design their own stars. Carle paints with his fingers and brushes using broad strokes before he cuts out the stars. Try this method, or cut out stars and then decorate the shapes.

4.   After this activity, attach ribbon or strings to stars so that they can be hung from the library ceiling and later be taken home to hang in children's rooms.

5.   Give children star shapes cut from paper. Encourage them to write a "star message" to someone in their family or to a friend. The following examples might inspire you and the children with whom you work.

Star Messages

"My star message to you says, you are my hero. I am proud of you and all you have done for me. You are a good brother."

"My star is my grandfather. He tells me stories about when I was a baby and how he taught me to smile when I feel unhappy. It might help someone else smile."

"My little sister is my star. She takes my hand when she is afraid. This reminds me to watch out for her. It makes me feel important and needed."

"My mother is a star to me and to all our family. She cooks our meals and gives us a kiss every day. I am a ten-year-old boy, and I still like her to kiss me."

"My dad is my star. Since Mom died last year, he is my best friend. He lets me tell him what makes me feel bad. He is the best listener. I love him with all my heart."

6.   Read one or more of the following books next: *Abuelita's Heart, My Mama Had a Dancing Heart, My Wish for Tomorrow,* or *Rainbow at Night.* You can also choose any book that you have on the topic of being grateful for our blessings.

7.   After reading the book and letting children express their ideas, ask them to talk about blessings in their lives. What blessing or good thoughts might they share with a friend or family member? Show them a beaded blessing pouch that you have made. You will want to make several examples (you could have teen volunteers make them) to show to the children.

8. Tell children that people all over the world have been making beautiful pouches with good-thought messages or blessings written down and placed inside. The pouches cannot be opened, but the secret thought inside is meant to pass on blessings to the receiver. This is a powerful thing to do for someone you love.

9. Pass out the materials and invite children to write their messages and fold them closed. Place the message in the middle of a piece of fabric (wrong side up). Now add a matching square of fabric on top of the message (right side up). You have now made a little "sandwich." Sew around the outside of the square to close it up. Glue or sew on beads or one large bead.

10. An alternative way to make your pouch uses only one square of fabric. Put the folded up message in the middle of the square (wrong side up). Now gather up the fabric to make a little bundle. Tie a ribbon around the "neck" of the bundle. Sew several beads or one bead to the ribbon or the pouch itself.

11. Explain to children that the bead is important to this project. Our modern word "bead" was spelled "bede" hundreds of years ago, in Old English. At that time, a "bede" was a little prayer or blessing.

12. Tell the following story of the Beaded Blessings Project.

The Beaded Blessings Project

Just a few years ago, a woman named Sylvia Clark, who teaches at the University of Wisconsin in Madison, came up with a wonderful idea. She had studied art and was particularly interested in decorated jewelry and pendants from all over the world, especially pouches and jewelry that held blessings or secret messages inside.

Sylvia created a project called "The Beaded Blessings Project." She made little fabric pouches from beautiful materials, wrote a blessing or message to place in the pouch, and sewed up her pouch. She added beads and ribbons to each packet.

Soon people all over the United States and the world asked Sylvia to tell them about this project. Sylvia explained that these beaded blessings reminded her of similar items made in parts of Africa or the medicine bags made by Native American tribes. People began to make their own beaded blessings pouches.

Sylvia describes this activity as a way to "celebrate unity by being part of an art project." It reminds all of us that by creating beauty in our own lives and passing on good messages, we can remember to share what we have in our life with others of good will.

Dreams, Wings, and Wishes: Three Lessons for School Programs

The universal ideas of wings and dream interpretation appeal to children as well as adults. The books in this chapter's bibliography and activities that follow are fascinating lessons for children in school settings. Add stories and extend these lessons throughout the year and across the curriculum. These projects involve student writing, creative movement, thinking skills, and imaginative discussions.

Materials Needed

1. Music tapes such as Respighi's *Fountains of Rome,* Debussy's *La Mer,* and Handel's *Water Music* (Select different kinds of music that range from Native American flute music, such as that found on the CD *Gathering of Shaman* and Copland's *Fanfare for the Common Man.*)

2. A pair of purchased or rented wings from a costume shop or borrowed from a church (Find something sturdy and well made, rather than wings that look like a fairy princess. Older elementary children tend to laugh at silly, cute, or trivial-looking things.)

3. A small or medium-sized box, no larger than a shoebox, beautifully wrapped in an unusual paper with a slit cut on top

4. Handmade paper or beautiful colored papers and linen stationary cut into rectangles of approximately four by eight inches

5. Small-tipped markers or ink pens, art paper, paints, and brushes

6. Books listed in the bibliography, and referred to in the procedure section (*Between Earth and Sky, Life Doesn't Frighten Me, Wings.*)

Procedure

1. Read selections from *A Rainbow at Night* listed in this chapter's bibliography. If you cannot locate this book, look for another that contains children's thoughts and wishes.

2. Read *Between Earth and Sky* or another book of nature poetry. Choose your favorite selections, rather than reading the whole book.

3. Ask children to write down phrases, words, or lines that inspire them to create "word pictures."

4. Tell the children to look at their words and then close their eyes as they prepare for a "mind picture exercise."

5. Have children close their eyes as you play the music selected from the list provided here, or other selections you choose. Let them settle into the silence by dimming the lights in the room and cautioning them to remain quiet as they relax and let their minds empty of all distractions.

6. After a minute or two, speak softly, as you guide children to create "mind pictures." The sequence that follows should help children visualize a mountain retreat, a nighttime walk, and a scene in the desert. Pause between each sentence or phrase. Use the following script:

Mind Pictures

- Yesterday's leftover air tasted like brown dirt.
- Wake me when the morning light comes yellow over my head.
- Listen to the magpie scolding, scolding, scolding me.
- Smell the rain clouds hanging on my head.
- Taste the morning misting on your face.
- Rain blurs the sky outside my window glass.
- Ragged mountain edges cut the sky.
- Smell the purple growing around you. It tastes like violet soup.
- Grey blue sky covers my backyard.
- Afternoon breaks through a rainbow on top of my roof.
- Sunset blood spilled on the ground.
- Turquoise-lavender mountains shadowed twilight time.
- My dog shines through the night, silver streaking his back
- Hear the katydid, katydid, katydid break the quiet of the black night.
- I raise my arms so wide I touch the star on top of the hill.

After reading the mind pictures, ask children to open their eyes. Give them paper to write down their own sequence of pictures and then paint what they have seen in the outside world and in their community.

7. During a second lesson, begin by telling children that not all places are as peaceful as in the previous activity. Read *Life Doesn't Frighten Me* and *Wings,* both listed in the bibliography. Show the pictures in the books as you read because the illustrations are just as powerful as the words.

8. Introduce *Wings* by telling children that the author-illustrator of this book was still a teenager when he created this book. Myers knew about the character of Icarus from Greek Mythology. Icarus was given wax wings so that he could fly, but he was warned to not fly too close to the sun. He dared to go farther than he should have, thus causing the wings to melt, and the young man fell back to earth. In this modern story, Ikarus, an African American boy, is given wings to fly away from kids who shun him. Read the book slowly.

9. Add soft music as you introduce the next activity. Your rendition of "Wings in Three Acts" can be done as a movement exercise with each student miming the story the teacher or librarian is reading. Other approaches are suggested in the following script.

Wings in Three Acts

Act I

Stage Directions: Dim lights in the room. Ask students to focus on their own actions, not to look at anyone else, and to move gently around one another as they move through the directions you give them. Maintain the silence; this is an exercise in movement and mime. Use your face and body movement to interpret these words.

Introduce the story of Ikarus, a boy from the city, a boy of promise, a boy who will find strength. Tell children how Ikarus rises one dark morning and discovers he has wings.

Have children visualize how others on the street and at school react to Ikarus.

Now, tell them how Ikarus walks out of the room, out of the school, and into the schoolyard and then starts to rise into the air above the building. Ikarus waits.

Act II

Stage Directions: Bring the lights of the room back to the normal level. Ask children to volunteer for parts of the kids at school. Some kids will be "gawkers," others will hang their hands and turn away, one will be the teacher, and others will be neighborhood kids who taunt Ikarus.

Leader: Now that you have all chosen your parts, I will tell the story of Ikarus again. I will play the part of Ikarus. You can respond to what I say and what I do. Act according to the words I speak.

(*Kids take their parts. Next the leader takes all parts of the kids who gawk and taunt. All children move as Ikarus would under this pressure.*)

Stage Directions: Now that the participants have engaged in role-play and movement, give them an opportunity to create collage puppets inspired by Myers's art. Have students who are particularly artistic cut out shapes of Ikarus from black and white paper, and his clothes from red and blue paper. Mount these shapes on card stock and attach them to craft sticks. Select several "readers" to divide the story into several parts.

Act III

Leader: Our story is retold again. This time, puppeteers will hold up their stick puppets and do the action of the main character, Ikarus. Our storytellers will read the story. The rest of the audience will listen respectfully as the story unfolds.

11. After the performance students discuss what the play meant to them. What feelings did they experience in the different roles? With whom do they identify, Ikarus, the neighborhood kids, or the students at school? Why?

12. The next part of this lesson, held during the next class time or meeting, focuses on wishes students would like to share with the world. Read part of the book *My Wish for the World,* which shows children's pictures and wishes from around the world in celebration of the fiftieth anniversary of the United Nations. Note that the overriding message is the wish for peace.

13. Show children the wish box you have created. Brainstorm with them about wishes they would they like to place in the box.

14. Give students the unusual papers and pens you have collected. Instruct them to write down a wish in their own words. When each wish is written down, glue a one-inch strip of purple ribbon to each paper. Have students write down their first names on the strip and place the wish in the box.

15. Read the messages anonymously; between each wish, hum the first two lines of the song "Let There Be Peace on Earth and Let It Begin with Me."

Idea Springboards: Activities to Develop

Happiness Stew

Read the book *Abuelita's Heart* about the interconnectedness of all living creatures. Make a "stone soup" or use the recipe for "Happiness Stew" to join the group together. Then make a happiness mural with pictures, drawings, photographs, and words from the children about what makes them happy.

Riding the Tiger Story Game

After you read aloud Eve Bunting's book *Riding the Tiger,* have children form a circle. Ask who would like to be the first "tiger rider." Have that child stand in the middle of the circle and chant, "I am riding the tiger! I am riding the tiger!" The rest of the kids respond, "Ahh. Ahh."

The tiger child chants again with the group responding in the same way. One child calls out, "I'm afraid. Help me. Help me." The tiger child responds, "Not me. Not me." Another child calls out, "Come down. Help me." The tiger child responds in the same way, "Not me. Not me."

This action can be repeated one or two more times. Finally, the leader says to the tiger child, "I'm the tiger. I've got you. You'll never be free. I've got you. You can't leave me."

The children in the circle drop hands and reach out to tiger child as they repeat, "Don't believe him. Leave him. You've got to be free. You've got to be free."

Freeze action and discuss the feelings of the various participants with respect to their experiences. What does the tiger represent besides a ferocious beast?

Pink and Say: A Memory Circle

Read Patricia Polacco's *Pink and Say* aloud. Ask children to form a circle. Join hands. As the leader, join the circle. Ask children to carry on Polacco's request. Repeat the name of "Pinkus Aylee. Pinkus Aylee. Pinkus Aylee." Ask children to retell the story and ask them to suggest other ways we can remember Pinkus. What other ways can we remember injustice so that the future will not repeat the past?

Resource Bibliography

The following professional resources and handbooks have been arranged according to the chapters to which they relate. I have found these books to be particularly helpful.

Introduction

Applebee, Arthur. *The Child's Concept of Story*. University of Chicago Press, 1978.

Nicholson-Nelson, Kristen. *Developing Students' Multiple Intelligences*. Scholastic, 1998.

Chapter 1: Red Hot Readers

Cullinan, Bernice E. *Read to Me: Raising Kids Who Love to Read*. Scholastic, 2000.

Fox, Mem. *Reading Magic: Why Reading Aloud to Our Children Will Change Their Lives Forever*. Harcourt, 2002.

Kohn, Alfie. *Punished by Rewards*. Houghton Mifflin, 1993.

Kropp, Paul. *Raising a Reader: Make Your Child a Reader for Life*. Doubleday, 1996.

Zahler, Kathy A. *50 Simple Things You Can Do to Raise a Child Who Loves to Read*. MacMillan, 1997.

Chapter 2: Art Smarts

Brookes, Mona. *Drawing with Children*. Jeremy P. Tarcher/St. Martin's, 1986.

Englebaugh, Debi. *Art through Children's Literature*. Teacher Ideas Press, 1994.

Silberstein-Storfer, Muriel. *Doing Art Together: The Remarkable Parent-Child Workshop of the Metropolitan Museum of Art*. Simon & Schuster, 1982.

Striker, Susan. *Young at Art: Teaching Toddlers Self Expression, Problem Solving Skill, and An Appreciation for Art*. Holt, 2001.

Chapter 3: Count Down

Braddon, Kathryn, Nancy Hall, and Dale Taylor. *Math through Children's Literature*. Teacher Ideas Press, 1993.

Evans, Caroline W., Anne J. Leija, Trina R. Falkner, and Cherie Blackmore. *Math Links: Teaching the NCTM 2000 Standards through Children's Literature.* Libraries Unlimited, 2001.

Hechtman, Judi. *Teaching Math with Favorite Picture Books.* Scholastic Professional Books, 1998.

Chapter 4: Food Feast

Barchers, Suzanne. *Storybook Stew.* Fulcrum, 1997.

Easy Menu Ethnic Cookbooks series. (Various authors and countries). Lerner.

Erdosh, George. *Food and Recipes of the Westward Expansion.* Powerkids Press, 1997.

Ichard, Loretta. *Hasty Pudding, Johnny Cakes and Other Good Stuff: Cooking in Colonial America.* Millbrook Press, 1998.

Irving, Jan, and Robin Currie. *Mudluscious: Stories and Activities Featuring Food for Preschool Children.* Libraries Unlimited, 1986.

Irving, Jan, and Robin Currie. *Second Helpings: Books and Activities about Food.* Teacher Ideas Press, 1994.

Kalman, Bobbie. *Pioneer Recipes.* Crabtree, 2000.

Chapter 5: Storytelling Sampler

Greene, Ellin. *Storytelling: Art and Technique,* 3d ed. Bowker-Greenwood, 1996.

Bauer, Caroline Feller. *Handbook for Storytellers.* American Library Association, 1977.

Bruchac, Joseph. *Tell Me a Tale.* Harcourt, Brace, 1997.

Dailey, Shelia. *Putting the World in a Nutshell: The Art of the Formula Tale.* Wilson, 1994.

Egan, Kieran. *Teaching as Story Telling: An Alternative Approach to Teaching and Curriculum in the Elementary School.* University of Chicago Press, 1989.

Hamilton, Martha, and Mitch Weiss. *Children Tell Stories: A Teaching Guide.* Richard C. Owen, 1990.

Rubright, Lynn. *Beyond the Beanstalk: Interdisciplinary Learning through Storytelling.* Heinemann, 1996.

Chapter 6: The Poetry Place

Bauer, Caroline Feller. *The Poetry Break: An Annotated Anthology with Ideas for Introducing Children to Poetry.* Wilson, 1995.

Fletcher, Ralph. *Poetry Matters: Writing a Poem from the Inside Out.* HarperCollins, 2002.

Janeczko, Paul. *How to Write Poetry.* Scholastic, 1999.

Livingston, Myra Cohn. Poem-Making, Ways to Begin Writing Poetry. HarperCollins, 1991

Parsons, Les. *Poetry Themes and Activities.* Heinemann, 1992.

Steinbergh, Judith. *Reading and Writing Poetry: A Guide for Teachers.* Scholastic, 1994.

Chapter 7: Barrel of Fun

Random House Book of Humor for Children. Random House, 1988.

Reid, Rob. *Something Funny Happened at the Library: How to Create Humorous Programs for Children and Young Adults.* American Library Association, 2002.

Chapter 8: Keen Jeans Booktalkers

Bodart, Joni Richards. *Booktalk! 3: More Booktalks for All Ages and Audiences.* Wilson, 1988.

Freeman, Judy. *Books Kids Will Sit Still For: The Complete Read Aloud Guide.* Bowker, 1990.

Freeman, Judy. *More Books Kids Will Sit Still For: A Read Aloud Guide.* Bowker, 1995.

Langemack, Chapple. *The Booktalker's Bible: How to Talk about the Books You Love to Any Audience.* Libraries Unlimited, 2003.

Littlejohn, Carol. *Talk That Book: Booktalks to Promote Reading.* Linworth, 1999.

Chapter 9: Hooray for the USA

Curriculum Standards for Social Studies. National Council for the Social Studies, 1994.

Fredericks, Anthony D. *Social Studies through Children's Literature.* Teacher Ideas Press, 1991.

Fredericks, Anthony D. *More Social Studies through Children's Literature.* Libraries Unlimited, 2000.

Grun, Bernard. *The Timetables of History.* Simon & Schuster, 1963.

Keenan, Shelia. *Scholastic Encyclopedia of Women in the United States.* Scholastic, 2002.

Sonneborn, Liz. *The American West: An Illustrated History.* Scholastic, 2002.

Chapter 10: *Heart to Heart and Hand to Hand*

Arnow, Jan. *Teaching Peace; How to Raise Children to Live in Harmony without Fear, without Prejudice, and without Violence.* Perigee, 1995.

Carter, Jimmy. *Talking Peace: A Vision for the Next Generation.* Dutton Children's Books, 1993.

Edelman, Marian Wright. *The Measure of Our Success. A Letter to My Children and Yours.* Harper Perennial, 1992.

Livo, Norma J. *Bringing Out Their Best: Values Education and Character Development through Traditional Tales.* Libraries Unlimited, 2003.

MacDonald, Margaret Read. *Peace Tales: World Folktales to Talk About.* Linnet Books, 1992.

Norfolk, Bobby, and Sherry. *The Moral of the Story: Folktales for Character Development.* August House, 1999.

Index

About the Author

JAN IRVING is Youth Services Supervisor of Pueblo City-County Public Library District.